THE ROAD HOME

Five True Stories
of Catholics
Who Returned
to the Church

Mark Neilsen

*To John,
With gratitude for
your friendship and
priesthood.
God bless,
mark*

LIGUORI
PUBLICATIONS

One Liguori Drive
Liguori, Missouri 63057
(314) 464-2500

Imprimi Potest:
John F. Dowd, C.SS.R.
Provincial, St. Louis Province
Redemptorist Fathers

Imprimatur:
+ Edward J. O'Donnell
Vicar General, Archdiocese of St. Louis

ISBN 0-89243-239-X
Library of Congress Catalog Card Number: 85-80930

Cover design by
Pam Hummelsheim

Dedication

For the Kopavi Community,
its roots and its branches.

Contents

Contents

Foreword

by Reverend William F. McKee, C.SS.R.

Pardon my enthusiasm. I loved this book!

It's thrilling to see Love meet love. To see Jesus touch people. To see them understand that, in spite of all, he loves them. To see their surrender to that love.

This is a book of high drama. It tells of fear, rejection, depression, pain, doubt, surrender, serenity, peace, and love. It's about the interaction between five immortal souls and their God. It has to do with raw emotions and distrusting, disillusioned minds which were turned off by an apparently uncaring God, or by a search for a God who would give meaning to their lives and peace to their souls.

In the past seven years I have worked exclusively with and for Catholics who have dropped out of the Church. I have touched and been touched — deeply changed — by more than seven thousand of these Catholics in the United States, Canada, and England. No matter what the country, state, or region, the stories I have heard in nose-to-nose, soul-to-soul encounters are recapitulated in these five stories.

When I first started working for the inactives I naïvely assumed that most of them were simply lazy sinners or people who were turned off by the laws on divorce and remarriage, birth control, and/or other Church laws. I knew that some had gotten a bad deal from a priest or a nun, that they were angry at God for the misery in their lives.

I soon learned how naïve I was, and that the "why" of the inactive Catholic was a very complicated question indeed. I began to realize that there were almost as many "reasons" for their leaving the Church as there were people. Most of all, I began to feel in my heart the goodness that most had in theirs, even though they do not go to church. That might seem a strange thing for a priest to say, but I know it to be true.

I was surprised to find a common thread running through the fabric of the lives of most of them: the thread of pain. Not necessarily pain that comes from the Church or Church laws or Church people, although I do not discount that. But pain that comes from life: from the death of a spouse, the death of a child, the death of a marriage, the death of a friendship; failures in business or in work; physical and mental illness; fear, doubt — "Why am I alive?" — "Where was God when I needed him?" — "Is there a God at all?" — and the myriad of other doubts and pains that afflict the human condition.

The reason pain is so important here is that it tends to erode self-confidence. Enough of it can sap faith in self and others, including God and Church. And in their pain they frequently turn away from God, who is the only one who can help them. It seemingly is a no-win situation if we do not take into account that this God of ours never lets go of us, no matter how hard we try to alienate him.

A baptized Catholic who has practiced the faith for some years cannot easily pull up his or her Catholic roots. In most of them, their Catholicism shows no matter where they go or what they do. It shows most dramatically in their hunger for the Eucharist and for Reconciliation. They miss a Church "that stands for something," a Church that outlines values to live and die by. Today I incline toward the dictum: *Once a Catholic, always a Catholic*. I can count on one hand those who, in my judgment, have lost the faith. The faith is not that easily losable.

Emotion rather than reason, heart rather than head, the subjective rather than the objective play a tremendous part in the decision — conscious or subconscious — to leave the Church. If the emotion is tied in with the emotions of childhood, the problem is amplified.

When I was in the seminary I did not look upon emotion in religion as necessarily being that important. Today I do. Today I believe that more decisions about religion are based upon emotion and feeling than upon reason-filled convictions. I have sat down, eyeball-to-eyeball, with too many people to believe otherwise. And by no means am I denigrating their emotions and feelings. They, too, have divine stuff in them.

This book is a step forward in the understanding of the utter complexity present in most people who leave the Church. After they read this book, many parents, educators, and Church people will probably stop blaming themselves for the exodus of their children and parishioners. They will realize that they were only a part of the picture. For most, a very small part, if that.

Introduction

For many Catholics, describing someone as having "left the Church" has a chilling finality about it. After all, he or she has, on the surface of it, turned away from the source of life. Accompanied by the consternation and confusion of relatives and friends, an individual may become alienated after a long period of frustration and discouragement, or a moment of crisis may result in a sudden break. Perhaps most commonly, one simply drifts away.

We know a good deal about the reasons, amplified by various media personalities and writers, why people leave the Church: its moral code is "too rigid"; it has changed too slowly (or too fast); or one simply is no longer able to believe in God. The alienation of former or lapsed Catholics can seem quite complete in human terms, yet the parable of the Good Shepherd suggests the story does not end there: Jesus has an abiding and even aggressive love for those who turn away from him.

The stories presented in this book testify to the reality that ex-Catholics *do* return to the practice of their faith, sometimes at great personal effort and under the most unlikely of circumstances:

— A cynical and embittered agnostic suddenly becomes aware of God's presence during a celebration of Mass.

— A divorced man, wounded deeply by an insensitive cleric, finds the courage to forgive.

— An educated woman rejects the faith of her childhood only to embark on a search for God that leads her to see, far more profoundly than at first, how God is revealed in an ancient institution.

These moments of reconversion came about because God, sometimes quite obviously through other people, touched the hearts of these men and women. And they are not extraordinary people, steeped in theology or expert in Church history. Rather, they are very much like all of us who balk and turn from the invitation to full discipleship. What is extraordinary is God's active presence in the lives of today's people, a presence moving their hearts long before they become aware of it.

In some way, each of these individuals has found the Church quite indispensable as a result of their encounter with the Living God. Coming back to the Church has, therefore, meant more to them than simply attending Sunday Mass or accepting the Nicene Creed. Each has, in his or her own way, embraced the central challenge of the Church: to embody in history the love Jesus has for his people.

These five stories are offered, then, as small signs of hope in the power of God to renew not only our individual lives but our families, parishes, Church, and, thereby, the world today.

The Next Foothold

"Don't even talk to me about the Church," snarled the stocky forty-one-year-old machinist. "The Church ain't nothin' but a bunch of hypocrites as far as I'm concerned."

The intensity of the response caused Father Jim, the associate pastor who had organized the Divorced, Separated, and Widowed Catholics group, to back off. Lee Schellert, describing himself as a "fallen-away Catholic," had come to the group's meetings from a neighboring town. A quiet man, Lee seemed to have a gentle quality that belied a rugged build and eyes that were always on the alert for confrontation.

Father Jim had suggested that Lee think about coming back to the Church, and Lee bristled as he shot back his reply. The matter was dropped, but it wasn't forgotten.

Over the next six months, Lee appeared often at the group's meetings, and Father Jim came to know him as a man who had been divorced for about three years and had custody of his two teenage daughters. Single parenting was hard for Lee, but he labored at it, just as he worked at everything he did. A skilled machinist, Lee had been able to tear down and rebuild an automobile engine by the time he was twelve. At his job, he was qualified, as a result of a lengthy apprenticeship, to run every machine in the shop. He was an expert with his hands, which he used even in conversation, methodically making his points on his fingers.

As a regular parishioner, Lee had been a member of the men's club and was always available to help out on a parish fund raiser. Now, however, he was obviously very bitter toward the Catholic Church. Yet, he was just as obviously coming to the meetings of the divorced and separated Catholics because he wanted, needed, something from the Church. A few months went by, and then Father Jim decided to try again.

After a meeting of the group one night, Father Jim caught up with Lee in the parking lot. "I'd like to talk with you about your feelings toward the Church sometime," he said. The two men leaned against the car and talked for about an hour, and Lee cautiously opened up a little. They made an appointment to get together again, and that's when the whole story came out.

Early Memories

Lee Schellert begins his story with the Catholic marriage of his father, Henry Schellert. The marriage took place in 1932. Just one year later, Henry Schellert came home from work one day to find his bride hemorrhaging and very nearly dead. He rushed her to the hospital, where doctors were able to save her from the effects of an abortion. When he learned the cause of his wife's bleeding, Henry Schellert was shocked. Later, he would tell her, "If you don't want to have my children, then this ain't no kind of marriage," and the two divorced.

Two years later Henry married Edith, the woman who would

14

bear his children. Though she was a Methodist, Edith promised Henry that she would help raise their children Catholic.

As it turned out, Edith would have a large role in seeing to it that her son Lee and his older sister Helen practiced their faith, since their father worked third shift as a mechanic for Greyhound Bus Lines. Edith made sure that the children got to Mass each Sunday and holy day and that the family fasted and abstained from meat according to Church law.

For herself, Edith Schellert always fulfilled her Sunday obligation no matter how sick she might have been. She worked in the soup kitchen at the parish school so that the schoolchildren might have a bowl of hot soup to go with their sandwiches at lunchtime. Whenever the parish had a fish fry, she was there dishing out coleslaw or bent over hot oil, frying the fish to a turn. She helped clean the church, and was even made an honorary member of the Ladies Sodality. She was a model Catholic — except that she could not be a Catholic at all, for she had married a divorced Catholic man.

Lee's first memories of the Church stem from those days when he'd accompany his mother to the kitchen at St. Gregory's school and she'd have him wait for her in with the first graders until it was time to leave. There, he'd sit and answer catechism questions right along with the other kids, but it was not until third grade that he began to understand what the Church was all about. Lee could not fathom why he could go to Communion but his mother and father could not. Sister Ann Christine, a strict but compassionate woman, answered his questions and explained to him why his mother could not become a Catholic. He had mixed feelings about her answers: Why was it so important that he be a part of the Church if his parents were not allowed to be? Most of all, he feared that his mother might die without Catholic baptism and go to hell.

At the time, Lee didn't know that his parents had talked to the pastor at St. Gregory's about the possibility of his mother's converting to Catholicism and their marriage being regularized. The pastor, however, was not encouraging. In the first place, he said, annulments cost a lot of money to prepare. In the second place, annulments were rarely given to people who had married again.

When the Schellerts moved into a new parish a few years later, they talked to the new pastor, but his answer was no more encouraging. He didn't know whether they had a chance for an annulment, but he echoed the previous pastor in saying that it would cost a good deal of money. On a mechanic's salary, a lot of money would be hard to come by. When the chancery was contacted about the Schellerts' case, the message came back loud and clear: Don't even waste your time.

Meanwhile, Lee and his sister Helen dutifully went to daily Mass with their classmates, kept the dietary rules of the Church, and watched as their parents gave of themselves to the parish, Mom as a cook and fund raiser, Dad as a leader of the Boy Scouts and helping hand at parish activities. It never made sense to Lee that his parents were so much a part of the Church and yet not allowed to participate in its sacramental life. But then, neither did it make sense that he had to learn all the Mass prayers in Latin to be an acolyte and again in English for the classroom. His parents insisted that he practice his religion, and he accepted it.

Lee spent a good deal of time with his father, whether helping him work on the relatives' cars on his day off or going hunting for squirrel and rabbit. By the time he was in eighth grade, it was clear that Lee, like his father, would make a living with his hands. Since the Catholic high schools offered no technical training or manual arts, Lee wanted to go to a public high school. But his parents objected. Religion had to be considered, they contended. When Lee countered with more questions about why they couldn't participate fully in the life of the Church, they decided it was time he understood the full story.

Lee's mother and father went into the details of their situation. In the eyes of the Church, they explained, they were committing adultery, and the way to annulment, as they were told, was blocked by the fact that they hadn't enough money. Lee felt heartbroken, somehow tainted by his parents' irregular marriage. "I was ashamed because I had been brought up in the Catholic book, and now I felt no good," he would explain some years later. "The Church's own catechism was saying I was no good. It was like a knife had cut a very deep, long scar in me."

His parents finally agreed that Lee should get a trade-school curriculum from the public school, but they insisted that he attend weekly classes at the parish school of religion. It seemed a fair exchange, and Lee dutifully showed up each week. He found little of interest in the religion classes until a conversation was sparked by the election of a new pope following the death of Pius XII. Over in Rome at the Vatican the cardinals were assembled, and they had already taken three votes. But as yet, no white smoke announcing the election of a successor had arisen from the chimney of the Sistine Chapel, where the cardinals were cloistered. Lee's religion teacher, a priest, allowed that "there was a lot of politicking that went on with the election of a pope." Lee found that very interesting, and, after discussing the matter for two weeks running, he had heard enough.

According to what he had understood from his parents, money and clout were the keys to an annulment; and here was a priest of the Church confirming that politics and power played an important part in the selection of the most important Catholic leader on earth. After class, Lee went up to the priest and said, "The Church is a farce. It isn't really concerned about anything but the almighty dollar, and it just plays with people constantly." Furthermore, Lee announced, this was the last class he was coming to. When he made a similar announcement at home, later that night, Lee learned that his parents had other ideas. He continued to attend classes, but he was now convinced that the Church — which, to him, meant the clergy and the hierarchy — really revolved around raw power.

Marriage

After graduating from high school, Lee enlisted in the Air Force and was stationed at Lockbourne AFB outside Columbus, Ohio. There he went to Mass, when he could get a ride across the base or when it wasn't too cold to walk the four miles to church. He still went to Mass because he felt close to God, but he had no affection for the Church as such. At age nineteen he decided to get married, and he wanted a Catholic wedding. Having been raised Catholic, he felt it was "the thing to do."

In order to get married in the Church, Lee first had to obtain consent of his pastor at the base parish for a wedding at another church nearby. Since his fiancée was Methodist by baptism, the couple had to attend special conferences in the rectory prior to their wedding. His wife-to-be agreed to raise the children as Catholics — to her it really didn't matter one way or the other.

Their marriage was in trouble almost from the very beginning. The new Mrs. Schellert was involved in several affairs early on, but Lee was determined to make the marriage work. His commitment had been for life — for better or worse — and a marriage seemed to him like anything else: if you sweated at it long enough, hard enough, you could figure out a way to make it work. Only much later would it become agonizingly clear that his wife would never be satisfied with him, no matter how hard he tried to reshape himself in the image of her latest lover.

When Lee got out of the Air Force, the couple settled down and bought a house. By the time their first daughter was approaching school age, they had become involved in parish activities. From time to time, Lee would discuss his domestic difficulties with the associate pastor, Father Bill, who gave him encouragement to continue working on the marriage. Continue working he did, but the constant rejection he faced was rapidly wearing away his self-esteem.

For a brief moment, Lee had great hope that the marriage might be getting on the right track. As their daughter was about to receive her First Communion, his wife expressed an interest in becoming Catholic. Lee was elated; now they could be a Catholic family with a solid base on which to build their marriage. His wife actually took instruction and was baptized. But her motivation, she later revealed, was more social than religious. She had merely wanted to be able to accompany her daughter down the aisle at Communion time. Her approach to marriage changed not at all.

In the midst of his domestic turmoil, Lee's mother passed away on December 22, 1974, shortly after having been baptized and given the last rites. Lee was glad that his mother finally had her heart's desire, but it was bitterly ironic to him that she should be allowed to enter the Church only when unconscious and about to die. When the priest eulogized her at her funeral as ''a good Catholic woman,'' Lee was outraged. He believed that his mother had been denied her religion by the clergy because of money, and here was a priest saying what a fine Catholic she had been! It was just plain hypocritical.

With the loss of his mother and the torment he was suffering in his marriage, Lee sank lower than he'd ever been before. His relations with his family were strained to the breaking point. They knew something was wrong, but he wouldn't talk to them about it. Even his job was in jeopardy as his performance flagged — whenever he'd work nights, images of where and with whom his wife might be gnawed at his concentration. Lonely and miserable, he was hanging on by the barest threads of self-respect.

One day several months after his mother's death, Lee's older daughter, then eleven years old, looked up at him and said, "Daddy, why do you put up with Mom running around on you the way she does?" Her eyes showed the hurt over what her mother was doing and over her father's seeming inability to do anything about it. Something deep inside Lee went off. Perhaps hearing the question on his daughter's lips broke through a trance in which he imagined that the problems of the marriage were his and his alone. "Why do I?" he began to ask himself, searching deep down for some answers. He felt like he was mired in the sludge and crud down at the bottom of a barrel. Why was he putting himself — and his children — through this sort of agony?

Divorce

Lee decided to offer his wife a choice: she could have a husband, a home, and a family or she could have her freedom. He gave her sixty days to make her decision, hoping all the while that she'd choose him and the girls. He didn't want a separation or to be single again. But as the days dragged on, he learned that his wife was leaning toward filing for divorce. Lee was devastated. He needed to talk to someone right away, to find some support for the decision he was going to have to make, so he called Father Bill at the parish. The housekeeper at the rectory said Father Bill was out of town and would not be returning for two weeks; would he like to make an appointment with the pastor? Although he had never spoken to the pastor about his problems before, Lee desperately needed help. He made an appointment to meet with the pastor the following Wednesday.

After work that day, Lee drove over to the rectory and sat down with the pastor. Upon hearing that Lee was considering divorce, the pastor immediately launched into a lecture about how Lee had to "work to save his marriage." Lee countered with a detailed narrative of what he had done over the years, all to no avail. His wife was not interested in changing her ways, and he and his daughters were suffering enormously. The pastor pondered the matter for a moment, and then he said, "Well, perhaps it would be better for you and the girls to get out of that situation. But I want to caution you," he went on, "I am not condoning divorce; and I remind you that you cannot go out on dates with members of the opposite sex. If you do that, you will not be able to go to Communion or receive the other sacraments."

"Wait a minute," said Lee, stung by his pastor's words. "What do you mean by that?" He had come hoping for some support in this difficult time, and here the pastor seemed to be jumping to close him out of the sacramental life of the Church. "If I go out with someone, that doesn't mean I'm going to sleep with them. If I don't break the rules of the Church, why can't I go to Communion?"

"Because," rejoined the pastor, "if you go out with women, your thoughts will be on sex, so you should not go to Communion."

Lee could not believe his ears. It was as though he were experiencing the same sort of rejection by the Church his parents had experienced. His eyes narrowed as he said, "Just where do I stand here?"

"You can come to church, but as a single person you won't be a part of the parish family anymore," said the pastor. "You'll no longer be a total family."

"You're trying to sweep me under the rug," objected Lee. He understood the pastor to be saying that if he went through with the divorce he'd no longer be welcome at parish family-centered events. "If that's the way you feel about me being divorced, then you don't have to worry about me being in your church because I won't be back." Lee got up, walked out of the parlor, and slammed the rectory door.

Outside, he felt crushed. On top of everything else, now the Church seemed to want nothing to do with him. It was like he'd just been kicked in the teeth and stomped on. He went directly home and made a list of his priorities in life, and the Church came out on the bottom. He couldn't deal with God — he felt utterly abandoned. He had tried to get help from a priest and had gotten more grief. "I just don't need that right now," he thought to himself, and concentrated on trying to survive the coming days.

A couple of weeks later, the associate pastor from the parish stopped in to talk. But by then Lee had his defenses firmly set in place. "If God doesn't give a damn, if the Church doesn't give a damn, if my wife doesn't give a damn, then why should I give a damn about God, the Church, or my wife? Screw the whole damn bunch!" he told the priest. It would be a long time before Lee could get himself together enough to even begin thinking about his relationship with God and the Church.

The initial adjustment to divorce was excruciating. Whenever he left the house, Lee felt like people were staring at him, judging. He was no longer comfortable socializing with his old married friends, and when he did try dating he found himself unable to get serious about anyone. Moreover, he was suddenly a single parent. His wife had decided against seeking custody after learning that Lee would fight it with proof she had had men over to the house or had hired baby-sitters in order to go out while Lee was at work.

Parenting by oneself, Lee discovered, was no easy chore. He became involved with a group called Parents Without Partners, and found its rap sessions and family activities very helpful in sorting through his new role. Slowly, his life again assumed a smooth rhythm, and his self-confidence began to return. But the more he felt "back together," the more he sensed there was still something missing.

Lee noticed a void within himself, but had no idea to what it could be attributed. "It was as though you had a mountain eighty-five percent climbed," he can now explain, "and you look up and there's no place left to go, you can't find your next foothold." He had thrown himself into the task of rebuilding his life, but after he'd done everything he could, it still wasn't enough. A woman he was dating suggested he attend services with her at her Methodist church. Lee went, but the experience was somehow empty.

While reading the paper one day, Lee came across an item announcing the formation of a group for divorced, separated, and widowed Catholics at nearby Assumption Parish. Still bitter toward the Church over the way he had been treated, Lee nevertheless wanted support from the Church. He could not understand why the Church had seemed to reject him because of his divorce. Not wanting to open old wounds, he was cautious — but he was curious and wanted to know more.

Church

When Lee finished his story, Father Jim could only say, "Boy, I can really understand why you're so angry!" Lee had expected him to explain why he should forgive the Church and start going to Mass again, but that response was not forthcoming. Instead, Father Jim suggested they get together again to talk some more.

At their next meeting, Father Jim told Lee he ought to consider filing for an annulment, a suggestion that caught him completely off guard. "I went into my marriage for the rest of my life," said Lee, "and now I'm going to be allowed to go for an annulment when my father couldn't in his situation?" The whole thing seemed like a joke, and he said as much to Father Jim. The priest then explained that although there was no guarantee, Lee might have grounds for annulment; that while Lee may have entered marriage intending a lifelong commitment, his wife's actions seemed to show that she had not. Lee said he'd have to think long and hard about that one.

Father Jim then added, "Lee, I don't want you to get mad, but why don't you just try coming back to church when you feel like it, not because you have to." Father Jim noted that according to Canon Law, Lee could continue receiving the sacraments as long as he remained in the state of grace. "I can't explain why you were told you couldn't receive the sacraments if you dated," he added.

Lee knew that what Father Jim was saying made sense, but he still did not feel at peace with God. Every time he walked into a church, he felt as though there was a big "D" on his back, indicating to one and all that here was this divorced person coming to church. Coming to church was like banging his head against a wall; the congregation, he feared, would not accept him. Nevertheless, in search of an elusive peace between himself and God, Lee began to go to Mass on Sunday whenever he felt like it.

By virtue of changes that had been made in parish boundary lines, Lee was no longer in his former parish. He was now in St. Cletus Parish. The pastor there, Lee had heard, was sympathetic to divorced Catholics; his own sister's marriage had ended in divorce. Lee decided to meet with him "to give him the benefit of the doubt." He explained to his new pastor that he was divorced, that he went to Mass when he felt like it, and that he wouldn't tithe; but if the pastor was willing to accept him, then he'd give what he could afford. The pastor said he understood where Lee was coming from — his sister had many of the same feelings after her divorce — and said he was interested in working with the divorced ministry in any way he could.

Lee attended Sunday Mass at St. Cletus on a "hit and miss" basis for several months, still feeling alienated and judged by the people of the Church and still angry. One Sunday, however, he listened to a sermon about how the family had to be a united effort of husband and wife. It occurred to him that he wasn't very upset about the sermon, despite the fact that it had excluded him and his family. Instead, while he might have picked a more appropriate homily, he was in church, perhaps for the first time in his life, because he wanted to be — not because he felt he had to be.

"All my life I felt like I had to be there," he explained some years later. "I had to go to Mass every day before school and then on Sunday — I was so perfectly glad to see a Saturday roll around! But when I want to be there, then I feel I'm with God in thought and spirit. I pay attention. I listen to the homily and try to pick out something that will pertain to my life. Same thing with the Gospel and the readings."

The gradual process of healing in Lee Schellert's relationship with the Church came to a head in October 1983 during a "Beginning Experience" weekend. The Beginning Experience is a process designed for those who have been divorced, separated, or widowed for at least one year and who are ready to make a new start in their lives. Modeled after the Marriage Encounter weekend, the Beginning Experience includes large-group talks, small-group sharing, and time for writing, reflection, and prayer. Participants are encouraged to "deal with the skeletons in the closets," Lee has said, "as a way to heal and close the door on the past and open the door to the future." On his Beginning Experience weekend, Lee Schellert was determined to deal with some skeletons in his own closet.

On Friday evening of that weekend, Lee was up until two o'clock in the morning, talking with a priest, Father Dick, recounting his experience, and questioning why the Church had tried to sweep him under the rug and pretend that as a divorced person he no longer existed. Father Dick said he couldn't account for why Lee had been treated as he had by his pastor when he had sought help with his divorce. Instead, he put two questions to Lee: Why are you blaming everyone here, and your family and parish, for what has happened to you? Why are you blaming me and every other priest for what happened to your father forty years ago, and for what happened to you? "I am not that person you dealt with," said Father Dick, "nor is every other priest."

Father Dick went on to say that the future was in Lee's hands: if he wanted to continue to hold a grudge against the Church, then he could. If he wanted to change the relationship, then he could do that instead. Now that he had heard these questions, it was up to Lee to decide.

The next day and a half of reflection and prayer provided Lee an opportunity to take stock of himself. Despite a painful past that might have hardened him against really hearing Father Dick, Lee could sense some truth in what the priest had said. As he prayed over the questions Father Dick had raised, answers came to him. "It was just like someone had turned the lights on around me," he would say. Now he could see that he had been blaming a lot of other people for the feelings he had within himself. "Blaming the entire Church left me off the hook when, realistically, I was just as much to blame as anyone. I was holding them at bay from me. I could not let them come close."

Lee came off that weekend "like I was walking around on cloud nine." He had finally had the chance to deal with some very basic feelings, and healing had taken place. "It was as though the world had been lifted off my shoulders. Now I go to Mass every Sunday, and I'm there because I want to be. I'm not 'in love' with the Church — the pastors and the priests — but I respect the Church. I respect their thoughts as long as they respect my thoughts."

Ministry

Since that weekend, Lee has been very active in the ministry to the divorced. Recently, he completed a year as cochairman of his local chapter of the Arise Ministry to divorced, separated, and widowed Catholics. He is currently serving in his second year as archdiocesan representative to Region Nine of the National Conference of Divorced, Separated and Widowed Catholics.

Lee Schellert is also a member of the Beginning Experience team in his area, helping to conduct weekends for people attempting to put the past behind them. On those weekends, Lee once again tells his story, this time not to nurture a grudge but in the hope of touching someone else. Perhaps, Lee thinks, that might be a way to wring meaning and value out of an otherwise bitterly painful event. "If I can let another person know they're not alone or help them go through what I had to," he says, "then maybe that'll be the reason I had to go through my divorce."

More than a 50/50 Chance

If you ever meet Virginia Druhe, you are not likely to forget her. A tall, sturdy-looking woman in her early thirties, she dresses plainly in cotton slacks and, in colder weather, a blue hooded sweat shirt. She is soft-spoken and serious of manner as her eyes fix yours and seem to penetrate with the intensity of her conviction. She is adamant about the links she sees between faith and justice, and one less confident about how the Gospel is to be applied may find her intimidating. Yet, Virginia Druhe is out to browbeat no one, and in her own life she follows a more demanding discipline than she asks of others. If she is firm in the way she interprets the requirements of faith, it is perhaps because faith comes to her at so high a price.

It wasn't long ago that Virginia, despite eight years of daily Mass at St. Rita's grade school and a strongly Catholic background, felt utterly without faith. At school, it was obvious that Mass meant something to many of her classmates, and certainly to the nuns and priests. But try as she might, Virginia could never seem to "make contact." With effort, prayer became only more and more insipid. Her parents' faith was evident in the quietly eloquent way her father's eyes stayed riveted on the altar throughout Mass or in her mother's more verbal, often vigorously questioning, piety. Others might sense the presence of God, but by the end of high school Virginia saw religion as a collection of odd behaviors and creeds in which she personally could detect no meaning.

That realization brought no immediate crisis as she prepared for graduation. An active girl with a lively sense of humor, Virginia was certain that someday she would deal with the question of faith, but she found it easy to put off. Meanwhile, it was simple enough to avoid upsetting her parents unnecessarily, and Virginia continued going to Sunday Mass; she liked to sing at church, and lately she had even occasionally felt a sense of community with the other worshipers. She was content to drift, and might have done so indefinitely but for a spirit of adventure that pushed her beyond the ordinary routines of her life.

With one sister a year older and another a year younger, patterns were an inevitable and useful part of Virginia's life. The Druhe girls went to the same school, slept, dressed, and ate on the same schedule, and even worked for the phone company together when they grew older. Most of the time, Virginia was at ease within these patterns, but sometimes they became unbearably tedious. One summer, playing with her sisters and the other kids on the block grew so tiresome that she enrolled herself in a program at a nearby county park just for the change. Similarly, she embarked on a two-week trip to Mexico after high-school graduation and was exhilarated: she discovered another culture, another entire way of doing things.

Mexico, however, proved only a tantalizingly brief hiatus from the familiar. She enrolled at the nearby Catholic university, but continued living at home and working at her old job, so the whole thing seemed routine. Filled with classes she found uninspiring, her first year of college life dragged until a good friend suggested the two of them sign up for a university program offering a sophomore year of study in Spain. Virginia didn't spend long paging through the brochures before she decided that, if nothing else, Spain would be something different, a chance to see how other people lived. As events turned out, the year in Spain proved extraordinary indeed.

Madrid

For the first time in her life Virginia was away from home and on her own far more than she had anticipated. Within a few weeks of their arrival in Madrid, Virginia and her friend had a falling out. The American students there never really coalesced as a group; and Virginia could find nothing in common with the Spanish women in her dormitory — their major interests seemed to be clothes and boyfriends. With classes no more interesting than they had been in the States, and without even the distraction of her old job, Virginia sought in vain for some diversion from her growing loneliness.

She did not find the city of Madrid itself a congenial environment. Its chief cultural attraction was the Prado, an art museum specializing in sentimental premodern works. A North American woman abroad in the city was certain to be subjected to catcalls, propositions, and even occasional physical harassment from the Spanish men seemingly bent on living up to their macho reputation. Except for a few good restaurants, Virginia thought the city dismal.

Alone in this setting, and with a good deal of free time, Virginia was forced to come to terms with herself. That was no easy task. She was beginning to feel some urgency about choosing what she would do with her life, but she hadn't a clue where to start. Her "identity crisis" had arrived, far from family and the myriad of other relationships which ordinarily tell a person so much about who he or she is. Virginia coped by stretching out her activities, deliberately doing the simple chores of letter writing, laundry, and eating meals. She spent time planning out her schedule, slowly etching patterns of her own choosing onto her days. Whenever possible, she made trips into the Spanish countryside, so full of the charm and appeal Madrid lacked.

Yet, as Madrid revealed the seamy aspects of Spanish culture, Spain showed Virginia a side of her own culture she had not noticed before. American business and military personnel were there in numbers, and in this country of great poverty the Americans could always be found living in the best neighborhoods. Seeing this inequity and being accosted on the streets from time to time with shouts of "Yankee go home!" Virginia began to feel estranged from her own country. Unsure of herself and miserable much of the time, Virginia looked forward with great anticipation to going home in February for her sister's wedding.

Being home again was wonderful, but it provided no "answers" for her life. When people asked how the year in Spain was going, she found herself responding "Just fine," rather than going into the sticky truth of the matter. Only with her old friend Beverly from the phone company — irreverent and intelligent Beverly — was Virginia able to strike up some authentic communication. Yet, the trip home was good; for after she returned to Madrid, Virginia felt relieved. She now knew that the root of her discomfort was not the fact that she was away from home any more than going home again would bring an end to her confusion. It was an insight that brought comfort, small though it was.

There was also a measure of comfort in the tears that came so easily in those days. One afternoon as the rain beat down on Madrid, Virginia sought out the top of the elevator shaft in the dorm, a favorite retreat where one could at least cry in peace. Atop the stairs in that cinder block cubicle, she could look out the little window to her left and see the muddy streets below as she wept. On this particular afternoon, ordinary in every other way, Virginia was suddenly seized by the recognition that God did exist. She had not been consciously pondering religious matters, and was somewhat puzzled. But this experience of knowing for certain that there was some center to life, some abiding truth, presented her with a *fact*. It was not a fact that made her feel warm or cozy, but it did calm her spirits.

Certain now that God existed, Virginia grasped a fragment of hope within the many uncertainties she faced. If God was a fact, however, religion was still very much a question. One of the first steps Virginia took with her new awareness was to stop going to Mass altogether. She found nothing in the liturgy so true as what she had learned in the elevator shaft. Hers was an encounter with the transcendent God, not with Jesus, and she was only beginning to grope, slowly and painfully, for a way of living that would be consistent with that reality.

Back Home

Back in the States, back at home with her old job, Virginia settled into the old routines that took some of the edge off her restlessness. She continued to feel alienated from many of the dominant values of her culture, but she knew no one else who felt the same way. At first she went to church to make her parents happy. But finally she told them she could no longer do it. Her father, overcome with emotion, could only say, ''You are damning your immortal soul to hell,'' before he got up and left the room. Her mother listened without judgment, and in the end Virginia went her own way.

At the end of her junior year Virginia moved into an apartment with Beverly, a change that brought with it an invigorating sense of independence. The neighborhood was lovely, with a tree-lined city park nearby and adjacent botanical gardens where there was always something in bloom. School began to take on a direction. After volunteering as a tutor in an inner-city neighborhood, Virginia decided to work toward a certificate in special education. The course work was tedious, but she made the acquaintance of Claudia, another special ed major, who had a great influence on her. Claudia, a thoroughgoing hedonist, took very seriously her responsibility to enjoy the material world, carefully savoring each encounter with natural beauty, art, music, and good company. Claudia, Virginia, and several other friends routinely got together at the local tavern for carefree evenings of conversation generously sprinkled with pitchers of beer and shots of tequila.

Claudia's *joie de vivre* was a timely antidote to Virginia's sensitivity to the tragic nature of physical existence. Virginia was prone to pessimism, a disposition that was perhaps rooted in a childhood experience of just how fragile life is. She had the experience when she was just seven years old. Virginia's mother had given birth to her youngest sister, and the delivery had been difficult. Her father came home from the hospital that evening, and her aunt asked him how mother and daughter were doing. ''The doctor gives them a 50/50 chance,'' he replied. That her mother's life should hang so precariously in the balance seemed intolerably cruel to seven-year-old Virginia. To embrace life fully and enthusiastically, one needs to believe that the odds against a tragic outcome are better than even.

As the clock was winding down on her student life, Virginia would need her sense of life's goodness buoyed. Her student teaching experience made it clear to her that she didn't want to be a teacher after all. Worse yet, around this time an uncle committed suicide, and a friend had an abortion. Although ambivalent about the morality of abortion, Virginia felt a deep, visceral shock; the awareness that the baby would never be born was immensely distressing. Against the backdrop of these grim events, Virginia was even less certain that she could ever figure out a decent way to live her life.

She decided to postpone the decision by taking some time to travel after graduation. She spent a few weeks in New York, and went to a friend's wedding in Canada. There, she listened while some Mennonite friends talked animatedly about their experiences of working at a nursing home. It sounded intriguing; and, for lack of a better plan, Virginia decided to go back home and look for a job in a nursing home there. She soon found one, and she took to the work immediately. In contrast to her wrestlings with questions about life's significance, there was something delightfully satisfying about being able to hand a bedpan to someone who needed it. The atmosphere was stark in many ways, but it was real. The old people no longer had energy to spend on social pretenses; and the aides, most of whom were working-class black women, spoke their minds with a candor Virginia found refreshing.

Merton

Virginia knew that the job, a tonic though it was, would not fulfill her longing for a meaningful direction in her life. She felt herself in a holding pattern, circling around something important. She got occasional glimpses of it, but it was still waiting for her in the future. In December of that year after college, Virginia happened across a copy of *The Man in the Sycamore Tree,* a book about Thomas Merton. To her surprise and elation, Virginia discovered that Merton was asking the same questions of life that she was asking. Finally, here was someone who made sense to her. She avidly set out to read all that she could, beginning with *The Seven Storey Mountain,* Merton's autobiography.

On an intellectual level, Merton provided Virginia with the same kind of relief she found at the nursing home: the stark reality of human doubts, fears, and questions came out in the open. Merton wrote about the depressed conditions he saw in Harlem, about the atomic bomb, about all the things that chipped away at the human person in modern society. And Merton wondered how it was that all we call good and beautiful can seem to rest on a base of other people's suffering and death. Virginia's love affair with Merton soared until she reluctantly realized that he could see all that he saw and still go on because of his sense of humor and his belief in the Catholic Church. Of humor, Virginia had enough, but she couldn't follow him into the Church. It would be easy, comfortable, and secure to do it — but it would be a cop-out.

Gethsemani

Looking for some taste of what she had found in Merton's writings, Virginia decided to go to Gethsemani, the abbey in Kentucky where Merton had lived. She and Beverly took off work one Friday in March and headed off on a trip that seemed ill-fated from the start. An ice storm on the road from St. Louis slowed them to a crawl. It took them all day to reach Louisville. Then, the following morning when they traveled south to Bardstown, they received the wrong directions, and it took them almost until evening to arrive at the abbey. When they finally got there, they immediately discomfited the monk who met them at the gatehouse by requesting to see Merton's hermitage and other places inside the monastic enclosure. It was just not possible, the monk said, seemingly perplexed that they should even ask. At last, disappointed and frustrated, they went to the church to hear the monks sing Vespers.

They retreated to a motel in nearby Bardstown and came close to deciding to go home first thing in the morning. But Gethsemani seemed worth one more try. They rose early and attended the monks' morning prayer of the Divine Office. Afterward, they were descending the stairs from the visitors' loft when they were confronted by an elderly monk. The monk asked if they wished to attend Mass. After an awkward moment exchanging glances with Virginia, Beverly said yes, they would. She said it more to avoid hurting the old man's feelings than out of any desire to worship in that way. The monk ushered them into a small chapel and began to celebrate the Eucharist. Very quickly he realized from their halting responses that these two young women were not regular churchgoers. He asked them if they were Catholic, and they explained that they no longer were. After pondering the matter for a moment, the old monk pronounced that they should not go to Communion. That amused the two women, for they had no desire to do so.

After Mass, the monk brought them out some breakfast and listened to their story of the previous day's tribulations. He said he'd be happy to take them out to see Merton's hermitage just as soon as they finished eating. As they walked through the woods that day, Virginia felt a great peace in this man, the only one at the monastery who had been at all warm or welcoming to them. When they finally had to go back home, he invited them to come back in May and, if they wished, camp in the woods of the abbey.

Gethsemani Revisited

Virginia and Beverly did return to Gethsemani in May for five days of camping in the woods. After they arrived, they learned that the old monk who had invited them was a bit eccentric. Most of the monks regarded camping in those woods as too dangerous to be recommended to anyone. During this visit, their host grew increasingly petulant and quarrelsome — to the point that he decided to spend no more time with them. Meanwhile, some of the other monks, particularly the gatehouse monk whose name was Alan, had begun to intervene quietly, visiting more frequently with Virginia and Beverly and bringing them reading material.

It was a scene surely without precedent at Our Lady of Gethsemani: two young women cooking their meals under the trees that spread across the driveway to the main gate, with the monks hovering around them, trying to figure out what these curious visitors were really all about. Alan would talk to the two women at length as they cooked. Yet, he would never sit down and always appeared a bit uncomfortable. One day he asked them outright: "Have you come back to the Church yet?" They were amused, but they told him no, they weren't interested in returning. Nevertheless, Virginia was falling in love with Gethsemani; its daily rhythms of prayer and manual labor seemed to make it an island of sanity in an otherwise disordered world. For the very first time in her life, Virginia saw clearly how people's belief in Christ was transforming the way they lived. Not that there had been any defect in the lives of other Christians she had known; but in the monks of Gethsemani, Christian living became visible to her eyes.

Virginia left Gethsemani that second time filled with the conviction that if she could only be a monk, her life would finally be in order. The problems, she realized, were two: she was a woman, and she was not a Catholic anymore. But back at home she began reading a Psalm each day, and discovered that it brought her a feeling of peace.

Jesus and Community

Throughout the summer Alan wrote letters and sent books to Virginia and Beverly, and they in turn made plans to spend a week at Gethsemani in August. It turned out to be a week of intense struggle for Virginia. On the one hand, she wanted desperately to be Catholic, to share in the Church's prayer life and the common sense of purpose and destiny that marks a Christian people. On the other hand, she steadfastly refused to make a union of convenience with the Church. Either she would have to see for herself that the Church was both true and absolutely necessary or she would go it alone.

On Thursday of that week, Virginia had attended the singing of the noon Office and was seated outside when the cook came up behind her and asked, ''Do you want me to bring some lunch out?'' In that instant, Virginia came to know with utter certainty that Jesus did exist. Like her experience of God in Spain, this was a factual kind of knowledge. And as Virginia had always believed the Church follows from the existence of Jesus, her dilemma should have been resolved. But it wasn't. Intellectually she could accept the Church — but emotionally she could not yet embrace it.

It was Saturday, and she and Beverly were walking in the woods that circle the abbey. They were planning to go home on Sunday, and Virginia was absorbed in the pros and cons of her own decision-making when Beverly declared that she had decided to return to the Church. Involuntarily these words leapt into Virginia's mind: "You have no right to go back before me. I've worked much harder all these years than you have. I should go first!" Virginia gasped at those sentiments, horrified that she should begrudge her dearest friend's decision to go back to the Church. She cried, shaking with paroxysms of shame and remorse. She was barely able to explain to Beverly and Alan what the matter was. She had glimpsed her own weakness; and while it wasn't a pretty sight, it was true. It convinced her she needed something beyond herself if ever she was to rise above selfishness and do any good. She confessed to Alan that day and on Sunday went to Communion.

"Novitiate"

Back in St. Louis, Virginia steeped herself in the traditional Church cycle of prayer and worship. The Scriptures came alive in the daily readings as she freshly experienced the seasons of Advent and Lent. With new eyes she saw the liturgy redolent of the meaning she had never been able to get in touch with before. Seeking a place to worship, she found a small parish church in a run-down neighborhood, where she attended daily Mass as often as possible. Meanwhile, she continued working at the nursing home, devoured Merton's spiritual writings, and volunteered in the local United Farmworkers' boycott effort. It was a period of her life Virginia fondly recalls as her "novitiate," a time of preparation and prayer, a time of great happiness.

To Virginia Druhe, the Catholic Church was an expression of the unity Christ desires for his followers; but it was also an institution holding a vision of what life is all about, a vision that differs significantly from that of contemporary society. The Church spoke of compassion and community in the face of the relentless accumulation of military and economic might by the superpowers. Finally, Virginia had found a home, a place from which she could begin to build a life that might embody authentic values, that might mean something in the face of the world's manifold violence and oppression. Like the monks at Gethsemani, Virginia wanted to make her belief in the Gospel palpable through her life; she wanted to be a sign to the world of the reality beyond. At the center of that life was to be prayer.

Although daily Mass was very important to her, Virginia found quickly that it was not enough; she longed for the contact that prayer, nonverbal and in solitude, brought her. Prayer, she explains, is "like finding a place you can rest. It's like sitting on a rock, a good granite rock, hard and cold, but you can trust it." Out of a deepening life of prayer in the two years after her reconversion at Gethsemani, Virginia found herself drawn to move on. Beverly would be leaving soon to work on a community-organizing project in New York, and Virginia began thinking she would like to live and work more closely with the poor. But how? Where?

The Catholic Worker

The answer presented itself when a woman from Omaha came to town trying to drum up support for opening a Catholic Worker house in St. Louis. The idea was attractive — offering hospitality to the poor in a prayer-centered community. Virginia decided to give it a try.

The reality proved far more difficult — and fruitful — than she had ever imagined. Karen Catholic Worker House, courageously staffed by four largely inexperienced women, opened its doors to needy women and children in 1977. Deluged by the enormous need for emergency shelter in the city, the Karen House staff grappled continuously with the nitty-gritty of hospitality: faulty plumbing, community cars that constantly broke down in the worst possible weather, men armed with pistols coming to the house looking for their wives or girl friends, guests taking drugs, staff conflicts, meals that never took place, a clothing room forever in disarray, and various other plagues. The staff made little time for prayer together, and within a year and a half the community was strained to the breaking point.

Virginia, too, was nearing collapse. She identified with the car she had brought into the community as she watched it get beaten up and fall apart during that first winter. As she threw herself into the work, responding to one crisis after another, she lost the ability to predict such things as whether she'd be able to get a night's sleep, eat a decent meal, or get a few moments to herself during any given day. Her health deteriorated. Only prayer held her together, and there was precious little of that.

The community regrouped: limits were set, and new house rules reflected the staff's need for a greater degree of order. Community tensions were discussed and ultimately resolved when some of the staff opened another Catholic Worker House a few blocks away to offer hospitality to men. Virginia initially stayed at Karen House, but took more time for herself to spend in prayer. Gradually, she spent more and more time in solitary prayer, living for a time as a virtual hermit within the Catholic Worker community.

Despite the difficulty it has presented over the years, Virginia maintains that offering hospitality at the Catholic Worker has brought her immeasurable spiritual wealth. "I may have lost some control over my life, but in the process I've encountered at least a hundred people that I've come to know and love and who've loved me," she explains. "And because of them, I've experienced an explosion of meaning in the liturgy. I'd never go back to the other way of living."

Basic Issues

In addition to wrestling with the demands of living in service to the poor, Virginia has had to deal with a desire that has been with her since she left Gethsemani the second time. Returning to the Church eliminated one of the barriers to her becoming a monk, but it did not eliminate the other barrier. "My life is about incarnating Christ, and nothing else can give meaning to it," she explains. "I believe in the sacraments completely. Since the Eucharist is the fountainhead of any other way of incarnating Christ, why wouldn't I want to celebrate it?" Acknowledging the role tradition has to play in the Church, Virginia by temperament is not content with doing something simply because that's the way it's been done for years.

Having taken a vow of celibacy, Virginia believes she is genuinely called to formal ordination in the Church. Her hope is that Church leaders will seriously investigate the phenomenon of women across the country experiencing the call to priest-hood. And she hopes that Church leaders will stand with these women in their efforts to change Church policy. Meanwhile, Virginia remains faithful to the structure of the institutional Church because she is heartened by many recent changes and by the presence of other women and men who keep working to expand the role of women. Sometimes the struggle to make others see the issue as she does is enormously frustrating, but the anger she feels somehow keeps her trying to deal with it from within the Church. "I'm willing to be patient," she says. "I'm just not willing to ignore the problem."

Neither is she willing to ignore the problems she sees arising from the arms race and militarism. Through such nonviolent protests as tax resistance and refugee work, she has, at some personal risk, sought to express a faith-based opposition to public policy. In early 1985, Virginia left for six months in Nicaragua as part of the "Witness for Peace" program. (In this program, North Americans have gone to the areas of conflict in that Central American country to stand nonviolently with the people in opposition to U.S. support for the rebels there.) Her plans included extended travel in the region, in part for the purpose of visiting contemplative communities to learn from them how they combine a life of prayer with resistance to the society around them. By the time she returns to the States, Virginia hopes to have learned "a way to live in contemplative community among the poor with explicit resistance to militarism and inequality in our culture."

Into the Future

Never far from the edge of despair, Virginia Druhe manages to maintain a wry sense of humor in the midst of a variety of struggles. She is not sanguine about changing her society's value system. Nor does she imagine women's ordination in the Roman Catholic Church to be likely in her lifetime. Yet she persists. "I think God wants to have God's love known in the world where it is not known now. I think that's what God wants to do with me. Prayer is sustaining through the ebb and flow, but it's exceedingly difficult, all the time essentially. I just take one day after the other; I don't know if I'm being led or if I'm at a dead end.''

A few days before she was set to leave for Nicaragua, Virginia confided that she had brought her uncertainty and frustration to prayer. ''When I complain to God about how hard all of it is, God just listens and then says, without patronizing, 'Go ahead. Get it all out. I know it's hard, I know it's painful.' Eventually, God says, 'Can you notice there's more life around than there used to be?' And I do know there's more life now than there was for me five years ago. I wouldn't consider going back.'' Tempering the boldness of what she had just said, she laughed wryly and added: ''At this point, I'm not *too* interested in going forward either.''

But she did go forward, into a situation of uncertainty and danger, determined to seek out more of the life she had found.

The Ardent Antagonist

Guy Grace trembled as he knelt in church that morning ten years ago and waited to go to Communion for the first time in his adult life. He was swept by a surge of gratitude in the growing awareness of how so many events in his life had been leading him to this moment. He squeezed his wife Elaine's hand, remembering how she had put up with all his guff and had never given up on him. His hand still in hers, they approached the altar for Communion, much to the amazement of the parish priest who as yet knew only the unrepentant Guy. Though a decade has passed since this once-ardent atheist came back to the Church, his family still doesn't know what to make of him.

The Making of a Young Atheist

On the surface, Guy Grace, today a forty-two-year-old project manager for a large financial concern, was a most unlikely candidate for a reconciliation with religion. Guy felt rejected by the Church as a youngster, and his hurt quickly became anger. By the end of high school, he was a vigorous adversary of religious faith and particularly of the Catholic Church. A bright kid, Guy delighted in challenging believers to "prove there's a God," and then ridiculing their efforts unmercifully should they try. But as Elaine somehow sensed early in their relationship, Guy attacked religion and God not so much because he had rejected them but because they mattered so very much to him.

Many of the contours of Guy's pathway to faith were formed in the family frictions that shaped his early life. Mildred, his mother, was raised by her father and her grandmother, a flinty pioneer woman known to the family as "Ma." Ma, who had been tough enough to nurse herself through influenza, was a resolute opponent of religion, and Mildred herself was to have no interest in churchgoing.

Mildred's first husband was an instructor at a roller rink during the Depression. They had had two children when she discovered he was having an affair with one of his students, and the marriage ended.

During the war years Mildred married Guy's father, an ice company employee whose job was to convince people that a new invention called the refrigerator was an unreliable passing fad. Their marriage was short-lived; he left Mildred and Guy after just two years. Reluctantly, Mildred placed her two older children with relatives. Then, taking Guy with her, she went to live with her sister, Charlyn, in a distant city.

Charlyn had early escaped Ma's formidable personality as a result of a childhood accident that left her blind. Ma's solution to the problem was straightforward: keep her out of the public eye. But Charlyn's father mustered the gumption to stand toe-to-toe with Ma, and the girl was sent away to a school for the blind. There Charlyn encountered a man who took children at the school to Mass every Sunday. Eventually, Charlyn was baptized. When Mildred and Guy came to live with her, Charlyn somehow prevailed upon her sister to have Guy baptized. And later, when Guy began to attend public school, Charlyn arranged for a nun to tutor him at home in the Catholic faith.

Raised by the two women, Guy quickly became spoiled and irascible when he did not get his way. Once, his kindergarten teacher tried to punish him by spanking him with a yardstick and locking him in the bathroom. Guy broke the stick into little pieces and began flushing them down the toilet, a bit of defiance that almost got him thrown out of school. When his mother married a blind war veteran named Joe, however, Guy's days of ruling the roost came to an abrupt halt.

Originally, Mildred had introduced Joe to Charlyn, thinking the two of them might make a match. But Joe and Charlyn couldn't stand each other. It turned out to be Mildred who found in Joe a man she could marry and thereby bring her family together again. In short order Guy found himself with a step-father who was a very strict disciplinarian, plus two teenage siblings to contend with.

Joe had a particularly profound impact on Guy's life. Left sightless by a grenade in the South Pacific, Joe responded to his loss by becoming fiercely independent. He had to do absolutely everything himself. This even included repairing electrical wiring at home, although the only way he could tell which wires were hot was by grabbing them with his bare hands. An active man and an excellent swimmer, Joe had no time for a little boy. Guy longed for his attention and love, but what he got were reprimands and occasional spankings.

For Joe, marrying at age twenty-three and acquiring an instant family must have posed special problems of adjustment; new responsibilities were heaped upon the daily demands of being blind. His marriage was a fiery one, Mildred being better read than Joe and not shy about letting him know it. They wrangled endlessly. But when they had a daughter of their own, Joe gave the child all a father's affection, a fact that daily served to remind Guy of all that he was missing.

Charlyn's influence once again prevailed, and Guy was sent to a Catholic school after first grade. In the nuns of St. Wenceslaus, Guy met his match. Imposing in their full black habits, these Sisters of a German teaching order initially frightened Guy and settled him down in the classroom. His early encounters with the Sisters were largely positive, but later confrontations reverberated painfully with the rejection he felt at home. These later experiences would leave him feeling unwanted by the Church.

Guy became an altar boy and, like most altar boys, thought about being a priest. Some of the priests he knew seemed to care for people, and people seemed to care for them. Guy's attraction to the priesthood may have been largely sentimental, but it was very important to him at the time. When he confided to his seventh-grade teacher, Sister Adolph, that he'd like to be a priest, her response was tepid; she said that he ought to convert his "pagan" parents first before thinking about the priesthood.

In the evangelistic style of the day, it was not unusual for the Sisters at St. Wenceslaus to issue this warning in no uncertain terms: if any of the children's non-Catholic parents died without baptism, they would go straight to hell. Guy had heard the warning more than once. This one time he decided to do as Sister Adolph suggested. Initially, his mother listened sympathetically. But when he pressed her, she finally explained that the parish priest had told her she'd have to leave Joe and go back to her first husband if she were ever to become Catholic. That she would not do, and so the matter was dropped. As for Joe, he just made light of his stepson's suggestion.

Those last years of grade school were filled with the turmoil of being attracted to something that seemed to offer Guy no place. Though he continued to serve Mass, often volunteering for the early Masses, nothing he could do would erase the fact that his parents were not Catholic. Finally, one of the Sisters told him that ''priests come from good Catholic families'' and that, therefore, his destiny must lay elsewhere. To the young boy, the Church seemed to be quintessentially the nuns and the priests, and he was being told he didn't fit.

Guy's resentment brewed as he entered public high school, where the dominant attitude toward religion was boredom. One summer, goaded by his mother into reading *War and Peace,* Guy discovered a voracious appetite for books, especially books that seemed to discredit the claims of Christianity. Turning away from the Church that rejected him, Guy relished any work that argued Jesus never existed or that tried to prove Catholicism was stupid, evil, or wrong. If the Church was a sham, he wasn't going to be fooled by it any longer. Guy lashed out at believers he'd encounter, first baiting them into discussions and then mocking their faith. ''How can you believe something as stupid as that?'' he'd taunt. ''There isn't any God!''

Nonetheless, Guy was a popular figure in high school, and one night one of his friends surprised him with a blind date at a local ''teen town'' dance. Guy was irritated and decided he would ignore the girl all night. But, finally, he gave in and asked her to dance. Then he walked her home. Three years later Guy and Elaine were married.

Marriage

Guy had no money, so their courtship often involved his hopping a bus over to Elaine's and the two of them watching TV or just talking. Guy loved to talk, and Elaine was very impressed with how much he knew about history, evolution, the Bible — all sorts of things. She was not very outspoken as a girl; and when Guy would rail against religion, Elaine mostly just listened. Elaine was from an Italian Catholic family; but her mother was a convert who did not attend church regularly, and her father went to Sunday Mass perfunctorily. Though Elaine could not have put it into words at the time, religion was something very important to her; and when she and Guy began talking about getting married, Elaine made it clear that she wanted a church wedding. Guy gave in for reasons that were simple to understand: he loved Elaine very much, and if a church wedding meant something to her, he'd go along with it. Elaine should have no illusions about it, however; he still thought religion was nonsense.

For the first several months of their marriage, Elaine would cajole Guy out of bed Sunday mornings to go to Mass with her, but gradually the battle wore her down. Not until their son approached school age would they begin attending Mass together again, and then it was more to save their son the embarrassment of nonpracticing parents than out of any new religious fervor. Yet, Elaine's hunch that Guy was not the staunch atheist that he outwardly projected gained some support from two separate outbursts of his anger.

Anger at God

The year 1967 was an eventful one for Guy Grace. In January he and Elaine lost their second son just hours after the child was born. The pregnancy had been difficult, but the doctor had given them hope that the baby would be all right. Elaine and Guy were together in the recovery room when the doctor brought them the awful news. Elaine was crushed; she had not even had a chance to hold the baby. But Guy was outraged. He stomped into the corridor and slammed his fist against the wall, sobbing and cursing God. Elaine said nothing about it at the time, but she remembered the incident, wondering how an avowed atheist could be angry at someone in whom he didn't believe. When she brought up the incident to him some months later, Guy just shrugged the whole thing off.

Despite the tragedy of his son's death, Guy's life had taken a positive turn in 1967. Unaccountably, he and Joe began spending more time together. Joe would come over to Guy's house, and the two of them would do minor repairs together. When Guy bought a new Volkswagon, he proudly gave Joe a ride in it. And Joe took Guy over to show him around the hospital darkroom where the blind man worked. Suddenly, Guy began to feel like he had a father; for the first time in his life he sensed that Joe cared about him and about what he was doing. Even though it was not a deep relationship, Guy basked in his stepfather's attention.

If Joe and Guy had not grown close, would that phone call on Christmas morning have been any easier to bear? Joe had died of heart failure after waxing the bedroom floor, said the voice on the phone, and Guy's mother needed him. Against whatever anguish he felt, Guy mounted a steely self-control and went quickly to the support of his mother. When he arrived at her second-floor apartment, she threw her arms around him and wept, "What am I gonna do?" Guy remained at his mother's side throughout the next four days, making the funeral arrangements and sitting at the funeral parlor for long hours as Joe's relatives and friends trickled in from out of town.

As the ordeal wore on, Guy's stoical resolve began to crack. He cried as he passed the casket for the last time before the trip to the cemetery, and after the graveside service he exploded at his older half-brother. The half-brother had argued with Joe and had not spoken to him for months. Guy shouted at him: "You hypocrite! How dare you come here? You never cared about him when he was alive." Joe's sister Lena had to grab Guy by the neck and push him toward the car to ward off a physical fight.

Back at his mother's apartment Guy was composed as he and Elaine sat with his mother and Joe's two brothers and sisters, sharing the bittersweet memories of old days and happier times. When it was time to go, they said their good-byes and Guy started down the steps and abruptly sat down. "Damn you, God! How could you take him from me?" he began to cry. "Damn you!" Guy quickly worked himself into a fury. He punched out five or six of the verticle spindles in the banister before Elaine and his mother could calm him down again. But, as in the case of the anger he expressed toward God when his son died, this episode did nothing to alter Guy's assertion that he believed God was a fiction.

Contact with the Church

The Graces enrolled their son in the nearby Catholic school. They did it, Guy reasoned, because it would make Elaine happy; and, anyway, it was better than the public school. Now they began attending Sunday Mass once more. Yet, it was often a struggle just to get Guy, tight-lipped and arms folded, in the pew. "It's a lot of nonsense," Guy would tell Elaine; but eventually he'd give in, and that was enough for his wife.

Elaine became active in the Home and School Association, and Guy would often come late to her meetings on his way home from the night classes he was taking in accounting. He enjoyed watching the parishioners bicker at those meetings. He reasoned that he could help straighten things out, so he began to volunteer for some of the projects. Whether he ever straightened anything out is debatable, but his involvement did bring him into contact with the pastor, Father Ben.

Father Ben was a country boy at heart, unaffected by the trappings of his ecclesial status. Guy took to him instantly. One day he decided to let Father Ben know just where he stood on religion. "Father," said Guy, "I don't know if it matters to you, but I'm an atheist." Father Ben, his eyes atwinkle, just smiled and said, "Gee, that's kind of interesting. We ought to talk about it sometime." Guy was taken aback; it did not appear that Father Ben would be easily impressed with a sophisticated intellectual approach. Guy began reading the Gospels and asking the priest questions about them. He also began paying attention to Father Ben's homilies, long rambling discourses that were appealing not so much for what was said as for how it was said. In Father Ben, Guy saw someone whose life expressed what Guy was looking for: the pastor really cared for people, and they seemed to care for him.

Whatever the inner workings of grace might have been in his life during this time, outwardly Guy decided that being an agnostic was a more consistent position intellectually; he remained highly antagonistic toward religion and the Church. When Elaine would invite the parish priests over for dinner, Guy, much to her chagrin, would jump all over them. "How can you be a priest in this stupid Church?" he'd bait them, reciting the past and present foibles of the clergy and the institution. Eventually, out came the old standard: "Prove to me there's a God!" The priests put up with Guy because they liked Elaine, at whose patience and fidelity they marveled.

Perhaps Guy wanted the pastor to try to force him to return to the Church. One day he challenged Father Ben, saying, "You know, Father, I haven't been to confession since I was sixteen.'' Without twitching an eyebrow, Father Ben replied, ''Well, OK, whenever you decide to go, just let me know.'' Guy was silenced. He was prepared for any other response — particularly the kind that his seventh-grade teacher might have given him — but this was totally unexpected. Father Ben steadfastly refused to conform to the stereotype Guy had constructed in his adolescent bitterness.

Marriage Encounter

One of the associate priests in the parish had been involved in a Marriage Encounter weekend. He had found it worthwhile, so he scoured the parish for a couple willing to attend. He couldn't find anyone. Finally, he asked Elaine Grace if there was a chance that she and Guy might like to go. Elaine was interested in learning the Encounter's communication techniques. But Guy was suspicious: Was this some kind of religious program? He finally agreed to go, reasoning that, if nothing else, he and Elaine would have time for a few romantic moments together.

Whenever the topic of religion was broached on the weekend, Guy assumed his agnostic posture, inwardly smirking at how gullible all these people were. At dinner Saturday night he confronted one of the team couples, saying to them, ''Why are you wasting your time doing this stuff when you could be out somewhere doing something worthwhile?'' Elaine just smiled weakly and wanted to sink under the table. Even she could not have guessed what was percolating beneath Guy's skeptical demeanor.

The next day was Sunday, and that morning's session brought to a head years of struggle and tension. The talks that morning featured a priest on the sacrament of Matrimony and a team couple on their relationship to the Church. The husband, a man about Guy's age, told of the difficulties he had had with the Church over the years and of how he had finally come to see the Church as essentially the people in it. Despite its flaws, he said, he now saw the Church as an organization worth belonging to. Guy strongly identified with the young man, and his blood began to rise.

After the talk, the couples went off for a period of being alone together, and now Guy really dug in his heels. "This weekend is stupid," he thundered to Elaine. "They're trying to convince me that God is OK, that the Church is OK — and that's bullshit. They're not going to brainwash me!" Elaine pleaded with him to forget all that and to focus on their relationship and what it meant. But Guy couldn't let go. He felt he was being swept away, and he wanted to stand and fight. After a miserable session together, Guy and Elaine joined with the other assembled couples for a celebration of the Eucharist to close the weekend.

Still stewing from the argument he had just had with Elaine, Guy couldn't help noticing how much love there was between the spouses, and among all the participants. Simply on a human level, the moment struck him as special. All the couples were invited around the altar for the consecration, and at the kiss of peace there was a lot of hugging and good feelings being shared in the group. As communion time approached, Guy suddenly became vividly aware of how very much he loved Elaine and of how he loved the other people in the room. He remembered the nuns and priests he had known in his life, whom he had admired and loved; his memory was so intense it almost seemed to bring them into the room at that moment. Then a most remarkable thing happened.

Guy recalls it this way: "It was as if God just picked me up in his hand and he said, 'All I want to tell you, Guy, is that I love you,' and then he put me back down. I really felt enveloped by God's love. All of a sudden I knew who Jesus the man was, too. It was like he was there, standing around the altar with us."

As the priest came to offer him Communion, all Guy could think of was "I haven't been to confession in sixteen years," and he just shook his head. Tears began to flow down his cheeks. Elaine and a lot of the others were also crying. Guy's love for Elaine was heightened by his realization of the enormous part she had played in his life, constantly keeping after him, never giving up. Having experienced God, Guy had a strong sense that the Church *was* the people as well as the priests and the nuns, and he felt like he'd finally made it.

"I also felt that I knew Jesus, that he did die for us and he did love us," relates Guy. "I thought about all the reading I'd done about his life, trying to prove he didn't exist — that's probably where some of the tears came from. For all those years I'd been denying him and possibly helping others deny him."

Guy's moment of awareness of God's love seems to have been in preparation even during those years when he appeared to be moving farther and farther from God. In a moment, the vast edifice of argument he had constructed against religion was transformed. Evolution no longer seemed to disprove Christianity or negate the Bible; rather, it revealed to Guy God's great intelligence in creating a complex and ordered universe. The scandals and weaknesses of the Church's past and present were to him signs of growth that paralleled the growth he had experienced in his own life. Even Guy's understanding of his stepfather's death was gradually transformed into his seeing it more as gift than bereavement.

When Joe had died, Guy was angry over the fact that he had

finally established a father-son relationship with Joe only to have it taken away. Later, Guy would come to see the relationship they shared as much more important than Joe's death. "God didn't take my stepfather from me, he took my father," Guy would explain. "Finally, Joe had become my father, and I had that experience and memory to treasure."

As a result of their weekend, Guy and Elaine became very involved in the Marriage Encounter movement from 1974 to 1979, serving their region in a variety of capacities. In their parish, they worked on the liturgy committee. Recently, they have curtailed their outside activities in order to spend more time with their three children.

Restive and Hopeful

As strongly as Elaine and Guy believe in Marriage Encounter, their involvement was not without its difficulties. The Marriage Encounter community to which they belonged was broken up when six of the eight couples decided to give more of their time to the charismatic movement. The six couples left the Marriage Encounter community. Guy couldn't go along with them, in part because he was skeptical of charismatic spirituality, in part because he had just discovered an enjoyable experience of community and faith and was not anxious to go off in search of another. The collapse of their community left him hurt and somewhat bitter; it seemed that the Charismatic movement had "stolen" his friends.

Nor has parish life been entirely satisfactory. Father Ben and the associate pastors to whom Guy and Elaine had grown close were transferred to other parishes, and the new pastor has proven to be more of an administrator than a man of pastoral expertise. One incident early in the new pastor's tenure rocked the serenity of Guy's newfound relationship with the Church. The Graces had been out late one Saturday night, working at a church-sponsored dance. As a result, Elaine and Guy got off to a sluggish start the next morning and, uncharacteristically, the Grace family arrived at church after the entrance procession had begun. When the pastor used his homily to reprove people who came late to Mass, Guy began to smolder. He felt singled out, publicly chastened, and he resented it. He adamantly refused to take Communion from the priest; instead, he walked clear around the church to take Communion from another Eucharistic minister. As Mass came to an end, Guy vowed through clenched teeth never to set foot in that church again.

Elaine quickly took charge. She sent Guy home with the children and — over her husband's protests — went to see the pastor. As she waited in the rectory, visions came back to her from those years when Guy scorned religion and ridiculed the Church at every opportunity. Was it possible that some silly incident like this could set all that into motion again? Elaine didn't know, and she didn't want to find out. Her eyes filling with tears, she recounted to the pastor the story of Guy's life. Befuddled by all the fuss, the pastor asked, "Why are you telling me all this?" Elaine's simple answer hit home: "Guy thinks you singled him out because he came to church late, and because of that he doesn't want to come here to church anymore." The pastor assured Elaine that his homily had not been directed at the Grace family, sent a note of apology to Guy, and no serious rift materialized.

Guy is not about to leave the Church over it, but his parish life is not as vibrant as it once was; both he and Elaine miss those earlier days. They were advised by a priest friend to seek out more congenial liturgical celebrations at other parishes; but, as Elaine says, "You're always a visitor in another church. This is our home, and though we may not like everything about it, it's still home."

Nor has anything stirred up the exuberance in their lives that Marriage Encounter once did. Today that makes Guy both restive and hopeful. "The toughest relationships I have are with Jesus, God and the Holy Spirit, and with Elaine. But there is commitment in those relationships, and I believe that something is going to happen. God is going to want me to do something, and I know something is going to happen to push me back in there. That's probably what keeps me going through this time of having a parish that is very dull, very dull."

Guy's expectancy is enkindled when he looks back over a life he sees filled with people and events that drew him out, that gave him the opportunity to know God and respond. Admitting that he has a tendency to float along, Guy today is waiting for another event that can show him a direction to take, that will bring back the excitement he knew during those years of activity in Marriage Encounter and the parish. "I yearn for that again, and it'll be there," he says confidently. "I don't know what will bring it back, but it'll be there."

Just Another Catholic

Brother Vincent Gray had every reason to be furious. He had carefully prepared his initial lecture in world history to be especially stimulating to a class of sophomore boys. These boys, experience told him, needed to be convinced that studying the past could make a difference in their lives. But almost from the moment Brother Vincent uttered his first sentence, a tall, gangling student in the first row had been chortling to himself uncontrollably.

The boy, Jerry Meyer, could not help himself. Before him stood a rotund black man with gold teeth, speaking with such command of the English language and intellectual grace as Jerry had never encountered before. Yet, to this boy who had grown up in an atmosphere of intense racial animosity, the Brother looked like nothing so much as a talking orangutan.

The incongruity of it all produced tense laughter, which vexed Brother Gray considerably. Yet, this extraordinary man somehow understood that Jerry could use some help; so, during the course of that year he made himself the boy's friend and encouraged him to learn. Through Brother Gray, Jerry would find an introduction to the intellectual landscape; he would also gain an enduring friendship, in spite of the inauspicious beginning of their relationship.

School Days

Jerry Meyer was the epitome of awkward adolescence when he walked into Brother Gray's classroom that morning. He had already reached his full height of six feet four inches. His ears protruded slightly in an era of revealing hairstyles, and he had eyeglasses and a cowlick. Jerry was without the confidence to even speak to a girl. He had come to McBride High School, an institution of the Marianist Brothers, with little motivation and no goals for his life. What he did bring, however, was a genuine gratitude that he was able to attend a Catholic school.

Not that Jerry was a pious youngster, for he had little personal experience of faith. During his high-school years he'd set out from home on Sunday mornings in time for Mass, but would then take a detour to the doughnut shop to sip coffee and linger over the newspaper until it was time to go home. Like many a high-school boy, his most profound religious sentiments came on retreats, when guilt would drive him to the confessional from which he would emerge greatly relieved. It was not so much religious faith that attracted him to Catholic education as his own experience. In the primary grades he had attended both public and Catholic schools, and as far as he was concerned the Catholic schools had it all over the public.

For example, Jerry so despised Emerson School, where he attended fourth through sixth grades, that he regularly responded to sick call in the hope of being sent home. To enhance his chances of contracting an illness, he'd open his bedroom window in the evenings and let cold air flow over him as he played, sans shoes and socks, on the linoleum floor. A somewhat bookish kid, Jerry was castigated and even ridiculed by his teachers at Emerson for being a daydreamer. Cheating at the school was routine, to the point that one year the students filched the teacher's copy of the arithmetic book and copied their homework with impunity. There was something wrong, Jerry sensed, with that kind of academic environment.

A seaminess pervaded the school. In Emerson's Scout troop, when the boys divided up for games, they'd give their teams obscene names while unperturbed adult supervisors looked on. Many of the children at Emerson came from broken homes or had older siblings who'd dropped out of school and now spent their days pitching pennies on the street corner. Though he was from a working-class family himself — his father was a postal clerk — Jerry felt almost aristocratic at Emerson. Little wonder, then, that he was enthusiastic when his parents announced that he would be spending seventh grade at St. Mark's; it *had* to be better.

Jerry loved St. Mark's from the day he entered. The kids there were brighter, livelier, and the atmosphere of the place tingled with the expectation of propriety and the anticipation of fun. In the classroom, Jerry's teachers immediately picked up on his interest in reading, and they encouraged him. As a result, his confidence began to grow. The teachers were nuns who had a reputation for being strict, but their affection for the children was evident. Jerry had his share of brushes with authority — like the morning he laughed so hard when another boy had accidentally thrown a ball through a school window that Sister Mary Grace, the toughest of the tough, made Jerry help pay for it. Later in the year, Jerry was pleasantly surprised to find out Sister Mary Grace liked him!

Perhaps Emerson School simply reflected the malaise that had descended on the Meyers' neighborhood after World War II. What had been a stable, urban, working-class neighborhood — a classic American mosaic of Irish, German, and Jewish families — began to deteriorate when government loans fueled postwar suburban housing developments. Many of the area's steadier families seized the opportunity to better their positions, and in their place came black families that were less well-to-do. The result was bitterness and frustration, an atmosphere in which racism flourished.

Belonging to a large institution like the Church provided a sense of place in the community during that time of great uncertainty and flux. The time he spent at St. Mark's and, some years earlier, Blessed Sacrament School gave Jerry a positive regard for the Catholic Church. His positive attitude also derived from the tales his father told of growing up in a Catholic community. Those stories, with their excitement and romance, always delighted the boy. The Lutheran family his mother came from were affectionate and virtuous people, but by contrast with his father's family they were a bit staid and stolid.

The chance to go to McBride High School, then, was something Jerry prized, even before he made the acquaintance of Brother Vincent Gray, who was certainly one of the most important influences in his life. The intellectual sophistication that Brother Gray offered was attractive, and Jerry was flattered by all the attention his teacher was paying him. With Brother Gray's encouragement, Jerry joined the speech team and began doing original oratory, something he never would have tried on his own. His confidence began to build. But when Brother Gray suggested one day that he try to get in the honors program when he went to college, Jerry was stunned — he simply did not think of himself as that kind of student.

Another McBride teacher, Brother Albert Stein, had an important impact on the future shape of Jerry's life. Brother Stein was a virile English teacher who could as easily talk baseball as Shakespeare's sonnets. The man was living proof that a love of literature was compatible with a healthy masculinity. For Jerry, that helped legitimate his own love of reading. Brother Stein stimulated Jerry's interest in reading better books. Under his direction, the boy discovered the wonders of *David Copperfield, Ivanhoe,* and other classics.

College

With the intellectual nurturance of these two men, Jerry began to do well as a student. He became editor of the school newspaper in his senior year, and won a scholarship to St. Louis University.

Moving on to college, however, initially eroded Jerry's newly won self-assurance. He knew he would be competing with students from better educational and social backgrounds, which made him unsure how he would fare. Jerry's experiences that first year in college were another discouraging factor. His advisor told him not to bother, as a freshman, even trying to get on the staff of the student paper. Then he was accused of plagiarizing an English term paper. Though he was cleared of the charge, the episode left a bitter residue.

Meanwhile, Jerry was living at home — which he hated doing — and working at a grocery store to supplement his scholarship money. He socialized with friends from the neighborhood and wound up doing more drinking and driving than was healthy for a young man. Over the summer, before his sophomore year, he thought seriously about quitting school and joining the service. But he finally decided against it so as not to lose his scholarship.

At the beginning of his second year at college, Jerry made the fateful step of stopping by the student newspaper to see if they had any use for his help. They put him to work immediately, and it rapidly became apparent that he could write as well as anyone on the staff. After a semester, he was made news editor; the following year he became editor. Working with the paper's staff, Jerry came into contact with good students who were intellectually alive and with whom he could relate on the plane of ideas. His success on the paper also helped him land a part-time job as a night reporter with a local daily paper. With the salary generated by the job, Jerry was able to move into the dormitory at the beginning of his junior year.

Jerry's moving into the dorm precipitated something of a domestic crisis; his mother couldn't understand why he wanted to leave home. But the move opened the way for him to enjoy college life to the full. Right away he realized how much he'd been missing; dorm living brought a heightened sense of independence, opportunity for discussions late into the night, and camaraderie with bright, fun-loving friends. Particularly did he enjoy the company of the staff at the student paper. On more than one occasion, they passed around a whiskey bottle as they put the final touches on another week's edition of the newspaper and then strolled over to the girls' dorm for a moonlight serenade.

Nor did a more active social life hurt Jerry's performance in the classroom. When he graduated in 1962, he was awarded a Woodrow Wilson Fellowship for graduate study in English at the University of Minnesota. During the summer after graduation, he took a job in Des Moines, Iowa, working for the publishers of *Better Homes and Gardens*. Although his job was terribly dull, Jerry enjoyed the workplace, in large measure because it afforded him a chance for conversation with a co-worker, Gordon Greer.

Greer was a very bright fellow who had received a master's degree from the University of Pennsylvania and had once worked for *The New Yorker*. Jerry admired not only Greer's intelligence but his well-tuned sense of decency and responsibility toward other people. When in the course of their conversations it became clear that Greer had no religious beliefs whatsoever, it set Jerry to wondering: "If a person can be as smart and as good as Gordon without religion, then what the hell is religion for, anyway?"

Living outside the Catholic environment, and having gained in intellectual sophistication and self-assurance during his college years, Jerry complacently discarded Catholicism as one might slip out of an old shirt. When he reflected on his own religious training, its most prominent aspects were the sexual taboos and the lists of Church rules — mandatory Sunday Mass, no meat on Friday, the Easter duty — which seemed to have no connection to the rest of his life. He had no hard feelings toward the Church; he had hardly any feelings about religion at all. The Church had simply become for him irrelevant, something he found he could do quite nicely without.

Early Career

During the middle of his graduate year at Minnesota, Jerry realized he did not want to enlist for the long haul toward a doctoral degree, so he completed his master's that year and left school. Since he wanted to get married and did not want to be drafted, he decided to apply for the naval officer's training program. The Navy promised travel, something Jerry had always found appealing. His subsequent itinerary on a destroyer took him off the coast of Vietnam, where he shortly saw enough to conclude that the United States' war effort was a mistake. After his discharge in 1967, Jerry became active in the anti-war movement back home.

His first civilian job was with the same Des Moines publishing firm where he worked briefly after graduation. Neither he nor his wife were any longer interested in Catholicism, but they did want to explore some kind of tie to religion through which they could express their opposition to the war. They also wished to do something on behalf of race relations and civil rights, issues Jerry had come to feel strongly about. The couple began to attend meetings of the Society of Friends in Des Moines, a large Quaker group that was very active in opposing U.S. policy in Vietnam. Eventually, Jerry petitioned for admission to the Quakers and, as is customary, wrote a letter explaining why he wanted to join the Society of Friends. In that letter, he made clear that his interest in becoming a Quaker was based not on any religious motive but on the ethical and social values he shared with the Friends. On that basis he was accepted into the Des Moines meeting.

Finding his new job no more interesting than the previous one, Jerry opted for a reporting job at the *Des Moines Register*. His success there led him to apply for a position back home at the *St. Louis Post-Dispatch*. Jerry began working for the *Post-Dispatch* in 1969, and in many ways it was the ideal place for someone with his political predilections. An institution of progressive opinion, the *Post-Dispatch* provided him ample opportunity to crusade on behalf of civil rights and against the war. His work as a reporter drew professional praise as well as the accolades of a small but active liberal community.

By the early 1970s, however, Jerry's relationship with the newspaper began to sour. The job of a reporter was growing tiresome, especially after he spent 1971 at Harvard on a Nieman Fellowship for working journalists. Hoping not to be a reporter forever, he wrote a book during that year, but the project was not sufficiently remunerative for him to leave the newspaper. His break with the *Post-Dispatch* finally came in 1973. The paper had been shut down by a pressmen's strike, and the owners had fought the paying of unemployment benefits to its reporters who were furloughed during the shutdown. To Jerry, the attitude of the paper's reputedly liberal owners seemed hypocritical; he had always assumed he was more than chattel in their eyes, but their behavior now contradicted that.

Through assignments in the business section of the *Post-Dispatch,* Jerry had come in contact with a large local public relations firm. The firm offered him a position, and he took it. He was glad for the chance to leave the *Post-Dispatch,* and for the first six months the job went smoothly. Gradually, however, his ego was to come in for a terrible beating.

Disenchantment

Jerry liked the firm he worked for, but he found public relations work unsatisfying: he worked at getting publicity for businesses about which there was nothing particularly admirable or distinguished. To his journalist's sense, the work at times felt a little whorish. Moreover, now that he was no longer the influential reporter with a large institution to back him up, he noticed he was not being treated with the same deference to which he'd unknowingly become accustomed. People he had once thought of as his friends now had little time for him. Since he no longer represented progressive causes in his work, his professional life did not bring him the praise of the liberal establishment. With his new role, his place in the community was profoundly changed, and that realization was quite an awakening.

From his new vantage point, Jerry could see just how much his own ego had been involved in being a crusading journalist. The environment at the paper had encouraged a kind of self-congratulatory liberalism in which people rewarded one another for their bold political and social stands. In fact, Jerry now concluded, there had been nothing particularly heroic about espousing beliefs that won him the approval of everyone around him. He had been smug as a reporter, and suddenly he could see it.

Jerry became disenchanted not only with his past behavior but with a political style. Liberal causes had become chic. In 1967, the people in Des Moines, with whom he had been involved in the anti-war movement, were genuinely committed to their beliefs. But by the early 1970s, the movement had expanded to include many who were not so committed. Liberalism was fashionable; as fashions changed, so did the political mood.

To Jerry, no issue seemed more telling of the infirmity of current political trends than the legalization of abortion. Although he was without faith-based principles to buttress his opinion, Jerry was convinced that abortion represented an unwarranted assault on human life.

A deep unhappiness settled over Jerry Meyer. Having lost confidence in his own past, he was now uncertain about his future. An essential ingredient in his world view since college had been the notion that the universe might, for all he knew, have been created in no more than a fluke of circumstance, a chance event without lasting consequence. He now became uneasy with that notion. Not that such a possibility suddenly became frightening, but it simply did not mesh with his own experience. Amid all else that had changed around him, all that had proved so fragile and false, the realities of love and beauty stood out as abiding and true. His intellect rebelled against the proposition they were simply energy spasms of an indifferent universe. Yet, he knew of no spiritual or philosophical ground for such realities, and that disturbed him.

Feeling closer to a breakdown than at any other time of his life, Jerry was not content to remain fixed where he was. But neither could he find a path for himself. He was doing well in his career — he had been made a partner in his firm — but the work was trying and the pace hectic. He needed to get away from it all and try to gain some perspective.

Jerry planned a three-week vacation with his wife and children in a secluded villa on the north coast of Jamaica. Some friends who had traveled there recently recommended the place; and with reduced summer rates and another family joining them to share the costs, the Meyers decided they could afford it. It would prove to be an excellent bargain.

Relationship with God

Any quiet retreat would have had a salutary effect on Jerry's restless spirit, but Jamaica is a place of extraordinary physical beauty. The nearest hamlet was fifteen miles away, so there were never any people around the villa. Lush tropical vegetation, pure white sands, and crystalline water brimming with colorful coral formations and exotic fish made the place a kind of paradise overflowing with life. Jerry spent a week just unwinding and recapturing a sense of himself, then a week in contemplation of his surroundings. He spent hours snorkeling or sitting outside observing the endless stretches of beach, water, and sky while sipping freshly squeezed limeade made with local brown sugar. The vitality of the place was dazzling, and the mystery of its beauty reinforced his growing suspicion that the world was not just happenstance. "It can't be an accident," he told himself, "not beauty in such profusion." Although he experienced no single moment of recognition, Jerry Meyer was, for the first time in his life, beginning to establish a relationship with the God who had created a world that Jerry found so palpably true, beautiful, and good.

The final week of his vacation Jerry spent steeling himself to return to the old grind. To his delight, he was not so unhappy upon returning home. A lot of the issues he'd been struggling with — conflicts at the office and the like — no longer seemed so important. All his questions had by no means been answered, but he did experience a measure of certainty about his world. He began his first serious reading of the New Testament, searching there for some sense of who Jesus was. Half suspecting to find an ancient madman in the New Testament accounts, Jerry came to see Jesus as a deep expression of beauty and truth.

Tending his budding faith by himself, Jerry gradually came to believe in God, and was beginning to think Jesus might be divine. During this period of two years, however, he felt no urge to return to the Catholic Church. Instead, the biggest change he made was to take a job as director of external relations with the McDonnell-Douglas Corporation, a manufacturer of aircraft and aerospace products. Jerry admired the high standards of the corporation's leadership, and, although he was not entirely comfortable working for an arms manufacturer, he reasoned that since there were some circumstances under which the use of such weapons could be justified, then the process of making them could also be justified. Representing McDonnell proved to be far more satisfying than trying to get media exposure for the variety of clients he had formerly served. But as important as his new work was to him, the thing that would more profoundly affect his spiritual life was another vacation.

At a relative's cabin in a mid-Missouri resort area, Jerry spent his days swimming and fishing, then relaxing in the evenings by settling in with a good book. He had brought from home a volume written by a physicist on the physical origins of the universe, but he found the book impenetrable. In search of something to read, he perused the cabin's bookshelves and there found a biography of Edmund Campion by Evelyn Waugh. Being a fan of Waugh, Jerry picked up the book and found it to be a moving tale of Campion's life and great devotion to the Church. At the same time, Pam, Jerry's wife, had been raving about a book she had found on the same bookshelf, Thomas Merton's *The Seven Storey Mountain*. Finishing Campion, Jerry turned to Merton.

Jerry was struck by the similarities between Merton's life and his own, though he recognized that Merton traveled in more exalted circles than he had. But both had been confirmed secularists, writers, and social progressives. Merton, too, had grown disillusioned and unhappy with his world, finally discovering not only God but the Catholic Church. The lives of Merton and Campion drew Jerry into a reconsideration of his own relationship with the Catholic Church, and he decided to investigate whether or not there might be a place for him in the Church.

Catholicism

Jerry realized that, his years of Catholic education notwithstanding, he did not really know much about the Church. He decided to talk with a priest, but not just any priest; it was important to him that his encounter with the Church and its traditions be as straightforward as possible, and he did not want some "hip" priest bending the rules so he could slip into the Church through a side door. No, if he were going to return to Catholicism, it would have to be, as he would later write, "through the same Gothic arches by which I had made my exit a decade and a half before." Jerry knew just the man: Father Joseph McCallin, S.J., his former college history teacher.

Father McCallin was not an extraordinary intellect, but he had a gift for communicating to his students his love of the life of the mind and his appreciation for the grand sweep of human history. A bit of a character and old-fashioned in much of his thinking, Father McCallin good-naturedly expressed his conviction that not much of value had taken place since the Renaissance. Jerry had always found Father McCallin's expression of his view of the world appealing, even when Jerry disagreed with him. Father McCallin appreciated reason and yet was a traditionalist theologically, just the person to whom Jerry wanted to talk about the Church.

Father McCallin agreed to meet Jerry on Saturday afternoons, and for about a year their discussions ranged over a variety of topics. The center of those conversations was not so much dogma as Father McCallin's talk about the weaknesses of the Church and his belief in a loving and forgiving God. "It's no wonder the people of the Church are called the faithful," said Father McCallin, "considering that they have to put up with priests." Knowing its weaknesses, Father McCallin also understood that the Church had an amazing resiliency. As evidence of its durability and vitality, he liked to point out that "the Church is the only existing human institution to have known Caesar."

Jerry told the priest one day that he had observed some

people, people like Gordon Greer, who had no religious beliefs but were nevertheless more virtuous and ethical than many Christians Jerry had known. Father McCallin responded that maybe those people didn't need the Church, for the Church was a collection of sinners. For the first time, Jerry began to see the Church as an institution that met a human need. After one of those Saturday afternoon talks, Jerry concluded that the Church met one of his own needs as well. So, he made his confession to Father McCallin, crossed the street for Mass at the College Church, and has been, as he puts it, "just another Catholic ever since."

Jerry has participated in parish catechumenate programs, the St. Vincent de Paul Society, and is currently a regular lector and commentator at Sunday liturgies in his parish. He also founded a chapter of the Manresa Society, a group of eleven men and a priest who gather monthly for talks on spirituality and prayer. But more than what he has done as a Catholic, Jerry emphasizes what being Catholic means to him. It has made him, he says, a more happy, more whole person.

Formerly a confirmed agnostic, Jerry values the Church for three main reasons: its intimate links to Jesus, its formidable intellectual heritage, and its tremendous vitality. "Being a Catholic," he explains, "means being a part of the Body of Christ, having a formal and institutional connection to Jesus. The Church embodies the awareness that Christ comes into our lives through the people we encounter. That is where the Church's conviction of the sanctity of the lives of individual human beings comes from." One practical consequence of this conviction, Jerry believes, is the "Church's fundamental position on abortion, making it a citadel of sanity and humanity when the secular world goes nuts."

In addition to this rootedness in Jesus and resultant sense of human dignity, the Church's vast intellectual traditions are valuable to Jerry. "Once you assent to faith," he maintains, "there legitimately arise all sorts of questions that come down to whether or not this thing you believe is ultimately preposterous. I would not be comfortable in any church that had not dealt exhaustively and competently with such questions. The Catholic Church has demonstrated that its beliefs are intellectually defensible."

Beyond his appreciation for the faith and rational strength embodied in the Church, Jerry Meyer declares: "I just like being Catholic. I'm proud to be a part of the Church. What else has maintained its vitality over the years? It's too easy to lose sight of what a miraculous thing that is: the Church is over 2,000 years old and it's still capable of self-renewal and still producing saints." Jerry points to the U.S. bishops' recent work on questions surrounding war and peace and their work on the economy as examples of that vitality in the United States.

Jerry resents characterizations of the Church as "a tyrannical institution that expects its people to be robots. One of the things I find so appealing about the Church is that it holds the dignity of each individual person. I believe it's no accident that the one nation presenting the Soviet Union with unsolvable problems is Poland; the Catholicism of Poland has given Poles a sense of their own dignity which makes it impossible for them to submit."

In his own life, becoming Catholic has not led Jerry to discard social or political views. "I haven't given up anything by becoming Catholic. Instead, I've added to what I believe and given it a foundation. The secular liberalism I believed in was built on sand, and it crumbled under stress. A large part of being a liberal, to me, means taking an ethical approach to politics. But it's difficult to find a footing for one's ethics without religious faith. Where do values come from? Why does human life matter if we have no notion of its source?

"I still believe the same things about race and international relations as I did in the 1960s," Jerry asserts. "In an analogous situation, I'd do the same things all over again. The difference to me is that if I were asked why I believed those things, I'd have a hell of an easier time explaining why."

Don't Be Afraid
to Keep Struggling

Ten-year-old Terri Presson had been a normal, healthy child until Christmas Eve 1979. She had the stomach flu, but it was only the following morning that Joe and Jean Presson, who was four months pregnant with their third child, suspected something might be seriously wrong. On Christmas morning, Terri showed no interest in opening her presents. Jean called the pediatrician. When she told him that Terri was bothered by light and noise, she and Joe could hardly believe it when the pediatrician told them to take Terri to the hospital at once. By the time they got there, Terri was barely conscious.

Terri was given the Sacrament of the Sick that same day. Afterward, the priest who administered it, a friend of the family, went out into the corridor and cried. Terri's condition was diagnosed as Reyes Syndrome, and within two days she was being kept alive by a respirator. Jean and Joe remained with

Terri at the hospital. During the day they were comforted by friends who came down to be with them, but each night they were terrified whenever they heard a code being called over the hospital public address system.

On December 27, the Pressons gathered with their friends for Mass in the hospital chapel. Jean had picked out the readings for the liturgy: the Gospel of Jesus with the little children and Paul's exhortation in Romans to hope in what cannot be seen. At Communion time, Jean felt herself pulled by God deep into prayer. In her mind she continued to beg, "She'll be all right, won't she?" But in the recesses of her heart, God seemed to be saying that tomorrow would be a bad day, a very bad day, but that he would give her what she needed.

The following night, the doctor asked the Pressons for permission to take Terri off the respirator. Neither Joe nor Jean wanted to trap Terri in her body if there was nothing that could be done for her, so it didn't take them long to reach their decision. Furthermore, Jean fully believed God could save her daughter with or without the respirator, and she continued to hope. Terri's death that day left her numb, but with the continued support of family and parish friends she and Joe managed to get through those first difficult days.

When their second son, Joey, was born that spring, Jean found relief in caring for the baby and his many needs. Only a year after Terri's death did the full spiritual impact of what had happened hit Jean. "I'm back at ground zero," she told her spiritual director. "I can't even say 'Our Father' without being filled with tension, wondering if there is a Father." Jean had thought she was through fighting to find God, having won belief after six years away from the Church. This time, however, she would find her answers more readily, thanks in large measure to the struggles of the past.

Early Days with God

Jean Presson's initial steps along the spiritual path led her into a delightfully vibrant relationship with God during her schoolgirl years at St. Peter's Parish in Quincy, Illinois. She loved attending daily Mass with her classmates, for especially in the Eucharist God was like a magnet attracting her with warmth and gentleness. Even on Saturdays, she would go to church in the company of her older sister, Sherry. Sherry played the organ at the eight o'clock Mass and would sometimes buy Jean a doughnut on the way home.

Jean's idyllic devotion to God grew unchecked until, at age fifteen, she watched Sherry pack her bags and go off to enter the convent. The reality of religious life came home to Jean as she saw the unusual garb the Sisters wore, but it was those black oxford shoes which convinced Jean in a flash that she could never be a nun herself. Facing her own unwillingness to dedicate her life to God through a religious vocation, Jean began to suspect that perhaps she lacked ''the right stuff'' to love God genuinely.

Furthermore, it was not easy letting go of Sherry, the one person to whom Jean could readily talk about God. Their parents were faithful Catholics, but aside from family prayers not much was said about religious matters at home. When the family drove Sherry to the convent, Jean found the atmosphere of the place stifling. Later, she and the family would visit Sherry and sit on folding chairs in one of the little circles of families that dotted the gym floor on visiting days. On those occasions Jean had no opportunity to talk to her sister alone. It seemed to her that Sherry had lost her individuality and, with the other novices, had begun ''acting like a nun.'' It was almost as though Sherry had died, and Jean grieved for her. Unable to graciously accept her sister's vocation, Jean once more felt unworthy of God.

At the same time, she felt constantly pursued by God — painfully so, since she would have liked to make contact with God but didn't know how. It was like waiting and wanting to meet someone and not being able to. Once, on a high-school retreat, she even toyed with the idea of telling the retreat master that she wanted to be a nun just so someone would take her seriously and talk to her about God. She never did tell anyone that; instead, she responded to her frustration by trying to make God less important in her life. It was a tactic she would try again and again in her life before she would finally give up the battle.

Problems with the Church

Jean had always loved and respected the Church, but in college she began to consciously question some of the things she was being taught. During her junior year at Quincy College, she took great interest in a theology course on marriage. She and Joe, her boyfriend since high school, had begun to think seriously about marriage. Jean asked her teacher privately for guidelines as to when she and Joe would be committing serious sin in regard to sex. The priest answered that serious sin occurred when the male got an erection. Jean had grown up believing that to question anything the Church taught, and therefore anything priests taught, was itself sinful. But it seemed to her far too difficult to avoid sexual sin. Either she wasn't good enough to really care about God and be a Christian, she reasoned, or the Church was out of touch with her life.

The following year, Jean gained reinforcement for the latter view. A theology course she was taking taught that marriage is first and foremost for procreation and only secondarily for mutual love. If for some reason one must choose between those two ends, she was told, it must be for the former. Angry with the Church for saying something with which she did not agree, Jean was terrifically frustrated; more than anything, she wanted God in her life, but she didn't seem to fit the mold to attain her desire.

Despite her difficulties with theology, Jean relished her philosophy classes taught by one professor who propounded logical proofs for the existence of God. The intellectual integrity of those proofs greatly appealed to her, and she drew a good deal of pleasure just from listening to ideas about who God was. It gave her a handle on God, and thereby satisfied some of her own longing to know God better.

Shortly after graduation in 1966, Jean and Joe were married. The couple moved to Evanston, Illinois, while Joe finished his final year in engineering at Northwestern University. Away from home and on her own for the first time, Jean enjoyed being a homemaker and making all the decisions that come with being independent. Almost without reflection, she had decided the Church was wrong on the question of contraception and began taking birth control pills right away. Though she still considered herself a Catholic, the Church no longer occupied the central importance in her life it once had.

The following year Jean and Joe went off to Houston, where Joe was to spend the next eighteen months doing graduate work in computer science. Meanwhile, Jean taught music in a grade school which was in the midst of the throes of desegregating. The tone of the school year was set early when part of the kindergarten class walked out in protest after being assigned a black teacher. The school administration responded by moving the youthful protesters into a white teacher's classroom. On that occasion and others throughout the year, the only person to stand up to the prejudices of the other teachers and the administration was a fellow teacher named Ann. A Unitarian committed to justice and political action, Ann had the gift of being able to confront people gently and to challenge them with honesty and compassion. Jean was living in a racially mixed neighborhood for the first time and was becoming sensitive to the struggles of black people. Ann challenged her to become involved.

Jean tried to emulate Ann's way of bringing an issue to light. Noticing the number of "Wallace for President" bumper stickers in the parking lot as she walked to Mass one Sunday, she spoke to the associate pastor after Mass and suggested that he preach on the problem of racism sometime. No, he couldn't do that, the priest told her, because then people might stop coming to church altogether. Jean was angry and disappointed. Ann, herself pretty much of an atheist as Jean later learned, seemed a lot closer to truth and goodness than the people Jean was encountering in her own parish.

Another group of people with which the Pressons spent a good deal of time were Joe's friends from school, a bright bunch whose intellectual sophistication Jean found attractive. They were also, by and large, nonbelievers. When Jean tried to justify her own faith with proofs for the existence of God, learned in her old philosophy courses, Joe's friends easily shot the arguments full of holes. At about the same time, Jean read an article in *Time* magazine in which it was pointed out that papal infallibility had been formally defined only in the mid-1800s. Jean had not known that fact, and suddenly she felt like a dummy for not having questioned the Church more vigorously before.

Having already decided that the Church was incorrect about the morality of birth control, Jean wanted to believe the Church was essentially wrong in general. In the refusal of her parish priest to speak out against racism, she found proof that the Church was hypocritical. Jean saw no way to deal with that, and was inclined to reject Catholicism entirely. She had been brainwashed, she decided, and the Church was a fiction. Almost immediately, Jean began to confront an even more troubling prospect: perhaps there was no God at all.

Does God Exist?

Wrestling with the question of whether or not God existed, Jean kept thinking about the suffering she observed, especially in the lives of black Americans and in the Vietnam War. "Why," she wondered, "would God allow such things to go on if he were really a loving Father? And if he really is a loving Father, why doesn't he make it obvious to us?"

Such questioning brought Jean a lot of pain but no answers. Sometime in 1968, she quit trying to figure it out, concluding she'd never know whether there was a God or not. She had become pregnant in May of that year, and the Pressons were planning to move back to the Midwest in December. Jean turned her attention from religion to politics.

Soon after the Pressons moved to St. Louis, Terri was born; and Jean immediately became absorbed with mothering. The baby was baptized, more for the sake of Jean's family, who did not know she had stopped going to church, than because it meant something to Jean. She had effectively given up her search for God.

But then, one weekend when she was visiting her parents, Jean listened as her younger sister, Connie, told of attending a charismatic prayer meeting and praying in tongues. "Well, then, let's hear it," said Jean. To her astonishment, Connie proceeded to pray in tongues. Now Connie, like her older sister Sherry, was a very intelligent person. If Connie was praying in tongues, thought Jean, perhaps there was something to it.

Back home, several days later, Jean couldn't shake the impression Connie's praying in tongues had made on her. One night after Joe had gone to bed early, Jean went into their spare room, took out a book of pictures and Bible stories her mother-in-law had given them, and began to pray: "God, I think I've decided you're not there, so if you are, you're going to have to hit me with a brickbat so I'll know you're there. If you are, then I'll do things your way. But you'll have to let me know." Jean tried to pray in tongues. She felt an inexplicable rush course through her, and found herself praying in tongues.

Jean immediately woke Joe to tell him what had happened, and he was amazed. Curious about the phenomenon, Joe read up on the subject a few days later and discovered that glossolalia — praying in tongues — can sometimes be associated with schizophrenia or hysteria. Joe, who had also drifted from the Church, suggested to Jean that perhaps some part of her wanted very much to believe there was a God and was trying to convince her there was. No longer feeling the initial "high" of the prayer, Jean thought Joe might be right. Nevertheless, from the moment she prayed in tongues, Jean could never again entirely abandon her search for God.

From that point on, Jean's quest moved in cycles. She would devote all her energy to finding God, then burn out and drop the project for about three months before starting in all over again. At times during the next four years, she experimented with going to a prayer group. She even attended some services at Presbyterian and Baptist churches. But the experience always felt empty somehow. It left her unsatisfied. Despite whatever frustrations she might encounter elsewhere, Jean steadfastly refused to set foot in a Catholic church again.

As Terri's fourth birthday approached, Jean was losing heart, despairing of ever making contact with God. Then one night she and Joe went to supper at the house of one of Joe's co-workers, a communal place where blacks and whites socialized together. Jean met a young man there, a former seminarian, who told her that after leaving the seminary he had stopped believing in God; but now he was sure God did exist. Jean was thrilled by this news, for if he could move from doubt to certainty, then there was hope that she, too, might. But how? "Don't be afraid to keep struggling," said the young man. "I'm sure you'll come to know God, because he does exist."

Experiments with Church

Buoyed by new hope, Jean once again plunged zealously into the search for God, and things began to happen fast. Within a few days, two Mormons on mission appeared at the door. Open to hearing whatever truth they might have to offer, Jean invited the Mormons in. After seven or eight visits to her house, the two missionaries finished explaining the Mormon faith and invited Jean to join the Church of Jesus Christ of Latter-day Saints. Jean couldn't make up her mind, so they all fasted and prayed for twenty-four hours, but Jean was still unsure. The Mormons advised her to join the church anyway, so she decided to give it a try. After about two months, uncomfortable with the Mormon theology on race and skeptical of the faith's mystical bent, she gave it up without regret — at least, she reasoned, she had confidently eliminated one possibility.

Soon thereafter, Jean had a dream that deeply affected her and propelled her to start praying more regularly. In the dream, someone was knocking at the door, and, when she opened it, there was God, whom she had been looking for all along. So bright was the light that surrounded God that Jean fell back, and God entered, saying, "You've made some changes, and I have a present for you." Jean woke up and was elated by the dream, for it said to her that, even though she was still very confused and unable to sort out all the questions flooding her mind, someday she would understand. She began to pray in earnest, asking God especially for a church, some kind of community, because she knew she couldn't do it alone.

During this period, the Pressons' son Robbie was born, and they went to register as members of the nearby Catholic parish so that the baby could be baptized there. Although they had been living in the neighborhood some two and a half years, the pastor never asked them why they had not registered before. Nor, when plans were made for Robbie's baptism, did anyone ask either Jean or Joe about their own faith. Later, that fact would make Jean angry; if anyone had questioned her at all, she would have gladly talked with them. As it was, they went on with Robbie's baptism. But this time Jean did not go through the motions effortlessly as she had when Terri was baptized. This time she was filled with internal conflict and tension. As her mouth spoke the answers required in the ceremony, a voice within her shouted, "I don't know, I don't know."

Just in case she had been wrong to leave the Church, Jean was determined that Terri should at least be exposed to God and Catholicism. Despite her own confusion, she enrolled her daughter in the parish preschool and, in order to keep apprised of what Terri would be learning, volunteered to help out there as well. Since no one ever asked her what she believed, they hired Jean without learning that she did not practice the faith herself.

For the first time in a long while, Jean found herself once again among Catholics socially. Tired of looking around and praying for a community to worship with, Jean perked up when one of her new friends told her about St. Christopher's parish, a warm and outgoing place where the pastor regularly made visits to the people's homes. Jean was much impressed with the pastor's willingness to involve himself with the people, so she decided to check out St. Christopher's for herself.

When she arrived there one Sunday morning before Mass, Jean was greeted at the door of the church by the pastor and parish staff. Upon entering the church, Jean immediately felt that God was saying to her, "You have been asking for a community, and this is it, so take it or leave it." Though she was drawn to the place, Jean remained restless within herself; she could not fully assent to belief in God or Catholicism.

The Problem of Suffering

Still casting about for answers, Jean learned that her best girl friend from Quincy was undergoing a series of tests for a condition that was resisting diagnosis and cure. She went to visit Bev in a Quincy, Illinois, hospital. In the course of their visit, Jean poured out the saga of her spiritual meanderings and asked Bev if she, with all that was happening to her, believed in God. Bev said she didn't know what to think because she had prayed to be cured and, thus far, had not been. The two women made a pact to spend six months doing everything they could to make contact with God and, then, get together again to compare notes.

On returning from the hospital, Jean made an appointment with the pastor at St. Christopher's and, acknowledging her own uncertainty, asked to make her confession. The priest was encouraging. He helped her examine her conscience and advised her, doubts and all, to say a rosary for her penance.

Wanting to reestablish her relationship with the Eucharist, Jean began attending daily Mass. She was determined not to fear being seduced into believing a pleasant lie; she decided to just let herself go, confident that she would be able to judge for herself whether the Eucharist was just emotional hogwash or something real. Jean was beginning to feel sure that, whatever else happened, she'd end up believing in God when the six-month experiment was over. But she was still a bit leery about repeating the Mormon experience. She was not quite so certain about the Catholic Church as she was about God.

Trying to "cover all the bases," Jean became involved in a parish prayer group in order to pray for a cure for her friend Bev. But when she attended a seminar in charismatic prayer, she felt torn all the while. She regarded the charismatic message with skepticism, and yet she wondered if God hadn't used praying in tongues to draw her back to faith. Once again, the problem of suffering surfaced, this time in relation to Bev's suffering, and this time it was just as perplexing.

As the seminar was ending, Bev was admitted to a nearby hospital. Her illness had been diagnosed as pancreatitis and lupus. Jean visited her and, their six months being almost elapsed, asked Bev whether she now believed in God. Bev replied, yes, she did. Jean was flabbergasted. How could Bev, in worse shape than ever, now say that there was a God? Bev could not say why; she just knew. Jean left the room that day completely exasperated. She went down to the hospital chapel, raging within herself at God, "How can you do that to her? Just look at her! How can you do that?" Jean was on the verge of chucking the whole business for fear that religion was pushing her toward emotional and mental collapse. But she decided, for Bev's sake, to go to one more prayer meeting.

She chose a prayer group meeting in a neighboring parish to be assured of comfortable anonymity. Toward the end of the meeting, Jean went forward to sit in for Bev. Members of the group laid hands on her and prayed for a cure. As they prayed, a woman among them said in prophecy, "Stop turning your back on me because you don't understand my ways. Draw closer to me and I will let you know my will." Perceiving that message as meant for her, Jean at that point in her life decided to quit trying to understand and explain everything and, instead, to turn simply to God in faith. Bev would live several more years, mostly in hospitals. And Jean, released of the frustration of trying to get rational answers to all her questions, found her way fully back into the Church.

Society's Expectations

Jean subsequently became very active in her parish, playing flute in the choir, serving on the liturgy committee, and working with other parishioners to fight "block-busting" tactics by unscrupulous real estate agents in their suburban neighborhood. On the surface, all that activity seemed to testify to the strength of Jean's religious convictions. But events were to show her how much she was being driven, not by the deepest desires of her heart, but by what society expected of her.

Jean enjoyed being a mother, but at the same time she felt a desire to "do something" with her life. To her, that meant some kind of work outside the home. Joe, too, had found his way back to the Church and had become quite active, singing in the parish choir and serving on various committees. Excited by their involvement with the parish, Jean dreamed of having an impact on the whole diocese. One practical implication of such plans was that the Presson family had grown large enough.

They had often talked about Joe having a vasectomy someday, and one day in 1978 Joe told Jean that he had made an appointment so that they could talk it over with a doctor. After meeting with the doctor, they set a date for the surgery, allowing themselves a month to pray about it and think things over.

Vacuuming the rug one day, Jean decided that if she heard from the parish deacon that day she'd ask him for the Church's position on sterilization. Within five minutes the deacon called. Jean wanted very much to believe there was nothing wrong with sterilization. She told the deacon she wanted not a lecture but just the facts about Church teaching on sterilization. The deacon, a young seminarian temporarily assigned to their parish, met with the Pressons and helped them to understand just what the Church was saying. He made it clear that the final decision was up to Jean and Joe. The deacon gave them literature explaining the Church's position, and urged them to read and pray over it together.

The literature the deacon gave them indicated to Jean that the Church might be reaching the right conclusions, but the reasoning "seemed all cockeyed" to her. The documents read like dissertations. They explained that at one time the Church had permitted the castration of young boys to preserve their soprano voices, but that the Church no longer permitted that. The conclusions were based on complex psychological analysis, and Jean found the arguments for the position simply unconvincing.

Nevertheless, Jean continued to pray and mull over the question in her mind. Attending a weekend conference on social concerns, Jean decided to ask the opinion of a participating priest who was well known for his writing on faith and justice. "Can I trust what the Church says about vasectomy?'' she asked. The priest responded, but not with a well-constructed rationale. Instead, he related that when a friend had had a vasectomy and had told him about it afterward, ''it made my heart so sad.'' Try the Billings method of natural family planning for a year, the priest urged; pray about it, and then see what you think.

With this new perspective added to what they had already learned, and after a good deal of prayer and discussion, the Pressons decided to cancel the operation and take the priest's advice. Consequently, as a result of having conceived unintentionally, Jean was pregnant at the time of Terri's death.

''Even if Terri hadn't died, I would be eternally grateful to that priest,'' Jean Presson says. ''I didn't realize at the time how much I was going by what society was telling me I needed to do to be fulfilled. I think God just knew me better than I knew myself at that point. When Terri died, there was such a shuddering relief that we hadn't gone through with the vasectomy. It was then I realized how important mothering was to me and how much I loved it.''

God Had Been There All Along

That realization began to unfold more fully a year after Terri's death, when Jean was once again assailed by doubts about God. She was very suggestible at the time. She felt strengthened when she was with people whose faith was strong, but, with those who were themselves uncertain, Jean could feel herself crumbling. When the doubts came rushing in, she would think of the Eucharist. More than anything else, that kept her going. Plagued by the same old questions, this time Jean knew where to go for help.

Although working with her spiritual director did not seem to help, Jean learned by chance of a retreat center which offered the Nineteenth Annotation Retreat of Saint Ignatius Loyola's *Spiritual Exercises*. Consisting of daily prayer and a weekly meeting with a director, the entire retreat lasts for about nine months to a year and is designed to help people who are active in the world to see how God acts in their lives. In a coincidence Jean Presson finds most meaningful, she began her retreat on February 3, Terri's birthday, and ended it in 1982, one year later to the day.

The retreat finally gave Jean a structure for being taken seriously in her relationship to God. Through the course of the year she moved from doubt to confidence that prayer was indeed an authentic give-and-take with another person, not merely illusion or self-projection. The retreat climaxed in God's request to Jean to go back in her imagination to the time in the hospital when Terri was about to die. Jean was terribly afraid to do that. She remembered only too well how utterly abandoned she had felt, and she wondered whether calling that memory forth once more might not trigger the old doubts. Apprehensive yet trusting, she prayed as God asked.

When Terri had been taken off the respirator and God had not saved her, Jean remembered thinking to herself, "Of all the times I needed you, God, you weren't there." As she now went back to that moment in prayer, she imagined the hospital scene once again. But this time it was clear to her that God had been there all along, in the form of all the people who had been there, crying with her and Joe, and supporting them. "If Jesus had been there in the flesh," Jean would later say, "I think he would have been doing the same thing."

This awareness did not expunge the hurt nor did it reveal the full meaning of Terri's death. But it did set Jean in "truth and reality," she explains. "God asked something very hard of us, but gave us the support to go through it. One of the most important helps we had was each other and the sacrament of marriage. Another was the people of the parish who took such great care of us all that time. To follow God, I have to accept the ways he goes about doing things and use the support he gives.''

Through the retreat, Jean came to a radically transformed view of her own life. ''Before, I felt that I needed to do something important, to see some results on paper for my life. I became very busy, too busy, and perhaps it's an unhealed part of Terri's death, but I can still hear her saying, 'Are you going out again tonight, Mom?' I'm very careful about getting into other things now. I know the children will be little for only a short time, and there'll be gobs of time to do other things. I just don't want to lose this time with them, especially the family time in the evening when we're all together.''

Jean Presson does not believe it is axiomatic that all mothers should stay in the home. But having examined her own desires, she knows she wants to give a certain part of her life to concentrating on child-rearing. ''I don't want to get very involved outside the house while Michael's not in school,'' she says of her fourth child, now a toddler. ''My need is different now. I don't need to have that much outside stimulation because I am deeply convinced that having kids is just a terrific gift. It's really hard, but I like the challenge.''

At the same time, Jean still believes very strongly in working to bring about a more just society. ''Some people need to be out there changing the world, but I still feel like I'm changing it. I do truly believe that if for some reason I could *never* leave this house, God would still call me, I'd still respond, and the world would be changed. We're all connected in the Body of Christ and what each of us does has an effect on all the others, as well as those who'll come along after.''

Exactly what all the effects of our actions might be on the future of the world is of less concern to Jean Presson than it once was. "God can bring much more good out of our lives than we could ever imagine, and we don't need to see it. Sometimes, we can see it, even in the bad things that happen, things like Terri's death, which was awfully bitter. Joe and I had Terri in life and in death, and it forced me to see that what we do now is an eternal thing. Having a child is co-creating with God to make life, and not just life here but life forever. So, even if I had had one child, we and God made that child, and it feels important enough that if I never did anything else, I'd be satisfied to have been able to do that."

Other helpful publications

Books

THE CATHOLIC CHURCH STORY: Changing and Changeless
Popular, easy-to-read history details the tremendous impact the Catholic Church has had on the formation of world history. $3.95

CATHOLIC ANSWERS TO FUNDAMENTALISTS' QUESTIONS
Offers clear, accurate answers to a great many questions that sincere Christians ask about the Catholic Church. Topics include: Scripture and Tradition, Salvation, The Mass and Communion, and others. $1.50

REACHING OUT WITH HEART AND MIND
Five booklets that explore the traditions and practices of the larger Protestant Churches. $1.50 each
Series includes **Reaching Out to THE LUTHERANS, THE BAPTISTS, THE METHODISTS, THE EPISCOPALIANS, THE PRESBYTERIANS AND THE REFORMED.**

Pamphlets — 50¢ each

The Teaching of Jesus on Love and Nonviolence
Which Came First: Church or Bible?
Is the Catholic Church a Bible Church?
A Catholic Looks at Evangelical Christians

Order any of these books and pamphlets from your local bookstore or write to:
Liguori Publications, Box 060, Liguori, Missouri 63057.
(Please add 50¢ for postage and handling for first
item ordered and 25¢ for each additional item.)*
**For single pamphlet order, send 50¢
plus stamped, self-addressed envelope.*